AF593863

Those Swinging Years

Dear George
Hope you enjoy this
Book
musically
Alvino & Luise
Rey

Those Swinging Years

An Autobiography

Luise King Rey

Olympus Publishing Company, Salt Lake City, Utah

Printed in the United States of America

Designed by: Thomas M. Hartvigsen

Library of Congress Catalog Card Number: 83-61978
ISBN: 0-913420-23-9 HB
0-913420-24-7 SB

DEDICATION

To my children Rob, Liza and Jon who are still making musical memories.

And to Janet Peterson for her loyal support and help to make this happen.

Contents

FOREWORD

I have written this book the way I remember the happenings. My perception of my own life and the actions of those around me are my own. My sisters and others may have viewed things quite differently — but this is the way I saw it — those swinging years — those fabulous years — when we sang our way out of a depression, when our country fought a war with pride and when everyone listened and danced to the music of the big bands.

I'm glad to have been around in those great musical years. I am happy to see them coming back and to be a part of them now. May the bands play on!

INTRODUCTION

What am I doing on this Greyhound bus? It is past two in the morning. In the darkness I can see only shapes and shadows of the Pennsylvania landscape whirling by. The windows are fogging and the rain is coming down in torrents. The windshield wipers are droning back and forth like a metronome keeping time for the sleeping musicians. It is November and the countryside by day looks as bleak and barren as I had remembered it before the first snowfall of the winter.

I look at my elderly husband in the seat beside me. He is dozing and seems very relaxed. He should be tired, but I don't think so because he is enjoying what he is doing. He loves leading the big band and playing those great old tunes, such as "One O'Clock Jump," "Satin Doll," and "In the Mood." People never seem to tire of them. He's enjoying the enthusiasm and applause of the senior citizens who are packing the concert halls each night. He looks good for a man past seventy. Alvino still has a lot of dark hair and he hasn't become any heavier. He weighs about the same as he did when we were married forty-five years ago.

When our agent asked him if he'd do a month of one-nighters, he looked over at me and said, "Honey, I'll go if you'll go."

Me again? Heavens this will make it the third time around for me. In the forties, when we were kids, my sisters and I traveled and sang with Alvino's big band. Then we traveled again in the sixties with the King Family. After our TV show went off the air we toured again doing concerts all over the country. And now in the eighties, with the beginning of a return to the big bands, we will be making the rounds once more.

"Sweetheart, you know I'll go if you want me to go. We've never been separated except during the war, why should we let it happen now? Sure, I'll go — just one more time! We should be home babysitting our grandchildren but if the folks want you to play for them, why not?"

And now we have just finished a concert at Thiel College in Greensville, Pennsylvania and we're doing one tomorrow night at Dundalk, Maryland. It's a 400-mile hop between these towns so Willie, our bus driver, has decided to break the jump by going on for a hundred miles or so after the concert. It's a soggy, damp night, and it's going to be hard on him. Willie is getting along in years too. He keeps himself — and us — awake by spinning yarns of bygone days.

The hop tonight will be difficult for the aging girl singer. A featured singer with Tommy Dorsey and Harry James, she is making a comeback with our "Big Band Show." But she doesn't have a lot of better things to do. Two divorces and some disappointments with her children have left her all alone now. She could be sitting in her rocker watching TV, but instead she is singing her heart out on stage, and loving every minute of it.

The elderly boy singer sits across from her in the bus and he too looks pretty good. When he gets into his $400 fine-tailored tuxedo, he seems to turn the clock back 40 years and appears as the handsome lady-killer he once was. He's very happy to be back on stage — but he's especially happy even to be alive. He just recovered from a cancer operation.

There is a quartet of blacks sitting in the back of the bus — not because they are black — but because they smoke. The rule of the road is "no smoking in the front of the bus." The elderly boy and girl singers just can't tolerate it anymore. At one time they both smoked but that was yesterday and now their lungs just can't take it. The black male singers are loved by everyone and have made many hit recordings. They tell tales of the old times when they couldn't travel with white people or stay in the same hotels, or even play Vegas. Times have definitely improved for them.

The old folks are emerging from every place imaginable to see the "Big Band Show." They come from Warsaw, Indiana; Bucyrus, Ohio; Adrian, Michigan; and Gastonia, North Carolina. They come from Florida and California and Utah and Arizona. They come to the concert halls sometimes looking old and crotchety but they leave looking young and happy. The big band and those grand old times have made them feel good, have taken them back to the romantic, carefree days of their youth. The music helps them feel young again.

The audiences applaud and cheer and demand encores. They give the band a standing ovation following every concert. They rush backstage to ask for autographs just as audiences did in the early days.

Why this sudden enthusiasm and revival of the big band music? Have thirty years of rock and roll and now disco been enough? Have ears tired of the cacophonous sounds and now long for the pleasant, harmonious strains of the music they heard when younger? Have music lovers of the forties decided to assert their rights and demand the music they want? Oh, happy days — are big bands finally coming back?

1

The Golden Gate

> It was the best of times, it was the worst of times, it was the age of wisdom, it was the age of foolishness, it was the epoch of belief, it was the epoch of incredulity, it was the season of Light, it was the spring of hope, it was the winter of despair, we had everything before us, we had nothing before us, we were all going direct to Heaven, we were all going the other way.

It was nineteen thirty-two and Daddy loved to quote the classics, even if Dickens did not appear on the best-seller list.

The little, old Chevy, that we called Put-Put, came to a jerking halt. Alyce and I, sleeping in the back seat, awoke. We always did when the car stopped. As long as it was running, we slept. It was a little like a cradle. When we traveled with the whole family, Daddy would gesture and show us points of interest but most of us kids would be sleeping. It made him furious because, being a school teacher, he wanted us to be eager to learn about everything. He wanted us to know about this vast American land, about its rivers and its mountains, about the sky and the stars, about politics and history and music. However, the only thing that seemed to rub off on us very much was music.

But Daddy wasn't here now to interfere with our snoozing. We had slept practically the whole way from Salt Lake to San Francisco. We had thought of taking a Greyhound bus, but Mama didn't want us riding with all those strangers so Karleton, our oldest brother, chauffeured us in Put-Put. Maxine sat in the front seat with Karelton and it was her job to keep him awake. He was a good, experienced driver and lasted the whole distance to San Francisco. We girls hadn't learned to drive since Karleton began driving at age twelve. We didn't need to learn—besides—we liked it this way. Alyce and I could snooze and giggle and talk about boys. We even had a couple of *True Story* magazines we could read when nobody was looking. Maxine, who was our saintly sister, talked with Karleton about school and books and religion and everything nice she could think of.

We were driving to San Francisco at the request of the famous orchestra leader, Horace Heidt. He had heard our singing over KSL radio in Salt Lake and had wired us to come for an audition. He was to book us at the Golden Gate Theatre for one week and if he liked us, we just might stay on with his band.

"Well, here we are. Little old Put-Put made it to San Francisco. I knew she would. She's a good little old car." Karleton opened the front door and stepped out on the curb. He stretched and yawned and I could see his face and eyes looked worn and strained. He appeared much older than his 22 years.

"I decided to drive up to Van Ness Avenue. I thought we would have a better chance of finding a service station where you girls can change." Karleton knew San Francisco pretty well, having taken the ferry boat from Oakland many times when we girls were singing over KLX in Oakland.

"There's a Shell service station right there. We can go in and change," Maxine said as she reached for the suitcase lodged between Alyce and me.

"Boy, wouldn't it be great to have a hot shower. I feel like I haven't had a bath for weeks." Alyce loved her hot baths and was as fastidious as any girl I had ever known.

"We'll just have to splash ourselves with cologne and put on fresh makeup like they do in Paris, and we'll feel as good as new." The Pollyanna was coming out in me. If there were anything sunny about life to find, I'd find it. Miss Blue Skies herself. The rest of the kids in the family continually teased me about this. They thought I was too fanciful, too up in the clouds, and not practical enough.

Karleton carried the suitcase that held our clothes and Maxine carried the paper bag holding our hats to the door of the ladies' room in the Shell station. Alyce and I dragged behind.

"Don't take too long now. You know your rehearsal starts in thirty minutes," Karleton said. He knew his sisters could really take their time primping. He had spent many impatient moments waiting outside the bathroom door of our one-bathroom house. He hated it when we made him late for school and made no bones about telling us.

"We'll hurry. We know how important it is not to be late," Maxine said. "You just get back in the car and wait. We'll be out in a few minutes."

We didn't take long getting dressed. It was hard, though, not having a shower. We were tired and dirty, but we were young and could spring back easily. Alyce wanted to know if she had her hat on all right and I assured her she did.

"Does my feather hat look OK?" I asked Alyce.

"Oh, I think it's darling. You look like something right out of *Vogue*."

It was good to be reassured by Alyce because I knew she had good taste.

Maxine didn't say a word. She just kept getting dressed as fast as she could.

"OK girls, that's as beautiful as you are going to get. We've just fifteen minutes to get to rehearsal." Maxine always kept us right in tow. She was the conscientious one.

We climbed back into the car and as we were driving down Market Street, I started to think about Karleton. This may be the last time he would be with us. We wouldn't need him anymore. If things went well, we would be joining Horace Heidt and his orchestra and Karleton would be out of a job. He had played for us at KLX and KSL, but Horace had his own band. There would be no place for Karleton and we would miss him terribly. Karleton had been a stalwart big brother to us, almost like a father. As much as we adored being around Daddy, he was restless and sometimes undependable. But we could always depend on Karleton. It seemed he carried the weight of our whole family on his young shoulders. He was unselfish; whenever we needed him he was there — never thinking of his own life — just trying to help us with our careers. And now we were dumping him, just like that, without even considering what would become of him. "Karleton must be feeling really low," I thought. He was a very private person and didn't show his emotions very much.

He had talked about playing on the *Dollar Liner.* A couple of his friends were musicians and had played with the ship's orchestra. The pay was nothing, but it was a good chance to see the world. Maybe it would be a good thing for Karleton. It would be something to take his mind away from his sisters.

"Hey, here we are — Market and Golden Gate. I'll let you off right here and pick you up in a couple of hours. I'll drive out to Golden Gate Park and find a nice place for us to picnic on the tuna sandwiches Mama packed for us. Good luck, girls. I hope you knock 'em dead!" Karleton's voice cracked with emotion, although he tried not to show it.

As we walked down Golden Gate Avenue, we looked for the theatre and its stage doors. There was an odd assortment of buildings on Golden Gate Avenue, all connected together in San Francisco style. We weren't sure which was the theatre. We came to a double door, but it had no door knobs so probably was only an exit. That couldn't be it. We walked on a little further, past a little cafe called Pop's Sandwich Shop. We guessed this was where the vaudeville acts and the guys in the band came for refreshments between shows. Next to that stood a shoeshine stand and just beyond was the stage door. We recognized it because it said — "Stage Door" — in neat block letters. Beneath, it read "Authorized Personnel Only." The door was painted in railroad brown enamel and showed signs of many coats of paint. The theatre looked as if it had been around as long as vaudeville. We all heaved nervous sighs. I felt a gnawing in the pit of my stomach, just like I had when we entered new schools each fall. I never quite knew what would be in store. I knew Alyce and Maxine felt the same.

"Well, here we are. Here's our big chance. Hope we don't blow it!" I said looking at Alyce who was straightening the seam in her new, sheer black stockings.

"Hey, are my seams straight?" Alyce asked as she turned her back to me so I could get a better view of her legs.

Alyce looked sexy. There was no getting around it. Those black patent spike-heeled pumps and sheer black stockings made her legs look slim. Her new black and white print dress looked good on her, too. And the white floppy felt hat she wore on the back of her head was just right. But Alyce didn't need to worry about what she was wearing. The guys never got past those big blue eyes of hers and did she know how to use them! Besides, Alyce had an ability to converse that put everyone at ease and females, as well as males, seemed to gravitate to her.

Now me, I didn't look sexy. I was considered pretty and people loved my pale bluc eyes, but I was shy and reserved and quiet and hated to meet new people but I didn't have any trouble. Alyce would bring home the boys and sooner or later they would discover me, and I would have a steady boyfriend while Alyce was out playing the field again.

Maxine was different. She was more like Karleton. She wasn't as flippant as Alyce and I. Daddy called her the "Florence Nightingale" of the family. She was almost like a nurse for Mama when all of the babies were born. While Alyce and I were out flirting with the boys and harmonizing and listening to records, Maxine was home with Mama doing what was necessary, whether it was making bread, cleaning house or tending the newest baby. It was Daddy who insisted on our including Maxine. He said, "Girls, you ought to let Maxine sing with you. She's got a pretty soprano voice and she could carry the lead fine." For some reason we hadn't thought of Maxine joining us. We didn't know how she would fit into show business; she was such a homebody.

She didn't look too much like us, either. Her eyes were small and sparkly and almond-shaped (maybe it was the Danish blood in her), while ours were large and dreamy. Alyce and I looked so much alike that we were often mistaken for twins. Maxine was cut from another mold, but she was cute and certainly didn't lack for boyfriends. She was vivacious on the stage, too. She fit the act just fine.

"Don't you think we should say a little prayer before going in?" Naturally, that came from Maxine, the serious one, the eldest.

"Right here on the street? People will think we are crazy." Alyce didn't want to be laughed at. She needed to be accepted by everyone.

"Well, we didn't say it this morning," I remembered. We were too busy getting ready, too excited. Besides, Mama and Daddy weren't with us to remind us. When we were home, Daddy always gathered his family around for morning prayer. During breakfast he bored us with current events, editorials, and his comments. Over the breakfast table we had suffered through the depression, the stock market crash, the beginnings of Hoover's decline, and Roosevelt's rise to the presidency. At this time the election had occurred but President Roosevelt would not take office until the following March. The exciting events of the New Deal were ahead — but politics seemed irrelevant to three stage struck girls — that stuff was for grown-ups. Our major interests were our singing, boys, and big bands — in that order.

And now, as we stood outside the stage door, I said, "Well, if we're that set on singing with a big band, we better get the help of the Lord." Alyce had to agree and so we huddled together, pretending we were "girl talking" and said a little prayer. When we had finished, we gave each other a last once over.

I was wearing a grey wool bias-cut skirt with a three-quarter length jacket I bought at Lerners for nine dollars. I thought the combination a good background for my blue rayon blouse and feather hat that brought out the blue in my eyes.

Maxine, I suppose, looked the most stylish. She wore a navy blue coat-dress piped in white with a white cloche hat that hugged her head and showed off her Colleen Moore haircut. She had made the dress herself and it looked quality. Besides, Maxine was skinnier than either Alyce or I, and not as curvy. She did look smart.

"Well, here we go," I said and picked up Daddy's old briefcase filled with our new arrangements. "Let's knock 'em dead!" echoing Karleton.

As we entered the backstage of the Gate, a man running the elevator introduced himself as Joe. He had a leather hand which made me wonder how he had lost his own hand. Had he been in show business? Maybe a juggler, now demoted to running the elevator. I wondered if he missed the stage. He was friendly and nice and made us feel right at home.

"Horace said he was expecting you girls. He's down in the basement in the rehearsal hall with the band. Here, get in the elevator and I'll take you down."

Joe told us as we rode down in the elevator that the Gate was a four-a-day house. That meant they showed four movies a day as well as four vaudeville performances sandwiched in. The band rehearsed every afternoon and every night. We were soon to find that it was much like being in the army or even in jail, very confining. But at this moment we thought it terribly exciting and wonderful!

We entered the basement rehearsal hall rather timidly. I was holding on to the music case and thinking, "I hope the arrangements are going to be all right." They had been marked by Daddy — "andante con espressione," "allegro," "moderato," "vivace." He wanted the band to know exactly how these arrangements should be played. Daddy was a music teacher and had been formally trained at the Chicago Conservatory of Music. He had borrowed money to go shortly after his marriage to Mama. However, his musical studies were cut short by the arrival of babies — one after another — mostly girls. So he went back to Utah, back to teaching school where he helped his family with the sounds of music during all his spare moments.

As we began growing to be young ladies, we found our ideas about music were quite different than his. He wanted us to sing in beautifully "pear-shaped tones." He wanted us to sing Cadmun's "At Dawning" and McDowell's "To a Wild Rose." We didn't hold still for that. We liked jazz and the blues and the popular tunes of the day. Our kind of music got us the job at KSL which then led to the Golden Gate. Horace Heidt would never have asked us to audition for him had we been trilling "Ah, Sweet Mystery of Life."

When Horace saw us enter, he cut the band off immediately.

"Boys, I want you to meet the girls from Utah. These are the King Sisters and their singing is as beautiful as they are." He then turned to us and flashed his million-dollar, professional smile.

Horace was a very attractive man, tall, broad-shouldered, square-jawed, quite sincere looking, although on closer scrutiny his eyes had a slightly shifty look. We discovered later that when any of us talked with him, we didn't get to say much as he did most of the talking. He would look away as if he were "clocking the door" to see if anyone more important wanted to speak with him. He spoke with a slight stutter which gave him a folksy, humble manner that only endeared him to the public.

He had a beautiful tan that he kept up with the aid of a sun lamp when not on the golf course. His hair was slick and shiny with pomade. He had a clean-cut, collegiate look about him much like a football player. His nose looked as if it had been broken, but if so, it did not detract from his handsome, athletic, good looks. Later, we found out from the boys in the band that, during the twenties, he had been a football star at the University of California. A back injury had kept him from going into professional sports, so Horace decided, that the band business was as good a racket as any and determined to tackle it. He wasn't much of a musician, playing only a little "parlor piano." But he was a tremendous businessman as well as a fine salesman, so assisted by his good looks and outgoing personality, he was earmarked for success.

His band was what was called a "stage band." He accompanied the different vaudeville acts that appeared each week at the theatre, in addition to entertaining the audience with novelty numbers of the day. He had traveled with his band over much of the world including London and Monte Carlo before he settled down at the Golden Gate Theatre. His band included a mascot — a trained dog called Lobo — as well as a male glee club that not only sang but swayed and clapped their hands at a given signal by Horace. He had patterned his band somewhat after the successful Fred Waring aggregation.

His career had been successful, but now vaudeville was beginning to die. Al Jolson had helped kill it by singing on the silver screen for the first time in the sensational *Jazz Singer.* So now with the advent of the "talkies" and another new medium called radio, the American public, always so faddish, had switched its interests to these new phenomena. Horace decided to get off the road and come home to San Francisco and house his band at the Golden Gate Theatre. He was going to settle down for awhile to think what his next move should be.

To be anyone in show business, you had to be heard on the air. Horace decided to let Lobo, the dog, go and replace him with a girls' trio. He heard our trio singing over KSL and sent for us. We had a good sound, much like the popular Boswell Sisters whom we had copied when we were kids. We also had a beauty and freshness (people told us) for which Utah girls were famous. Horace thought we could enhance his band the way the Lane Sisters had added new life to Waring's band. The sound of a girls' trio was hot stuff and we would be a bonus to his band. Lobo would have to go; he had it all figured out.

When Horace introduced us to the boys in the band, they gave us a rowdy college boy welcome and we relaxed. My knees stopped shaking and I looked to Alyce who was giving them her best Rita Hayworth smile. She was also taking off her hat and shaking out her naturally curly brown hair so it wouldn't look too set. It didn't take Alyce long to catch on.

I looked at the boys in the band. They were dressed in cords and sweatshirts, which we later called grubbies. Why were we so gussied up? Why had we worn our best Sunday clothes? We looked stiff and overdressed like we were going to a ladies' tea. And the hats, why on earth had we worn hats? The boys were probably laughing to themselves.

I thought of the time we might have primped and fussed with ourselves getting ready for this morning. My new grey suit that I thought looked so nifty now suddenly embarrassed me. Alyce wasn't embarrassed though. She was laughing and making little wisecracks to the boys in the band and I noticed how they were eyeing her — especially the dreamy eyed trumpet player. Well, the hats at least, could go. I promptly removed mine and Maxine followed suit. I knew then we had much to learn about show business and what went on behind the scenes.

Horace gave the music to the piano player who passed it out to members of the band. Then he said, "From the top, boys," and they started playing, paying no attention to Daddy's academic markings.

After we had rehearsed our first number, the piano player, who was conducting the band for Horace said, "Is this next tune a direct segue?"

"A direct segue? What do you mean by that?" I flushed because I really didn't know what it meant.

"It means you go directly into the next tune without any announcements. Boys, get out your pencils, and we'll strike out all those classical markings and put in our own."

We were embarrassed. Daddy would have been hurt had he known they were undoing his painstaking efforts. We were soon to learn that musicians had a language all their own and it wasn't long before we understood it. Later when our parents heard us saying "hip," "solid," "groovy," "cat," "zoot," "cool," "corny," "icky," "give me some skin," "take five," and "blow" they would shake their heads in dismay. But we knew what we were saying; so did the boys in the band.

The rehearsal was OK. Horace was busy with secretaries and people interrupting him with business affairs. The pianist acted as the conductor and was kind and thoughtful and didn't embarrass us with too much hip musical language.

After we had finished rehearsing our last tune, Horace said, "Girls, I'm sorry we won't be able to have a dress rehearsal on stage. We're having a special early bird movie tomorrow and after that we go on cold with the stage show. You girls will go on right after the opening band number. That will be about one o'clock. You better get here by eleven. Joe will show you your dressing room. It's going to be great. You will love our audiences at the Gate."

As we walked out of the theatre, Alyce said, "How does he know it's going to be great? He didn't hear us sing. He was talking business all the time!"

We were a little nervous about that "no dress rehearsal on stage," but I, the Pollyanna, said, "Oh, it's going to be fine. Didn't you think the rehearsal went well?"

"Oh, it went all right, but I sure wish we hadn't been so dressed up. How embarrassing." Alyce was still worried about making it with her peers.

"I wonder if Karleton is back yet. We were in there two hours. I hope he didn't get tired waiting."

I knew Maxine was concerned about Karleton.

Karleton was there right where we left him, waiting patiently in Put-Put. "Well, how did the rehearsal go?" he asked as he opened the car door for us.

"It went fine, just fine!" I spoke up before Alyce could spread her gloom around. She got discouraged very easily. She was like Daddy in that way. I thought there was nothing to get discouraged about. Horace and the boys had really been very nice and friendly to us.

We climbed into the car and Karleton started the motor.

"I'm starving. Who's got the tuna sandwiches?" Alyce and I spoke in unison. We were hungry.

"I've got them and they are going to stay right up in front until we get to the park." Maxine was faithfully following Mama's instructions: "Eat in that beautiful Golden Gate Park and pretend you are having a picnic. It will make things more pleasant for you."

It wasn't very pleasant, and the park didn't seem very beautiful. It was cold and damp and the San Francisco fog started rolling in with such density that we had to eat our dessert (fig newtons and bananas) in the car, despite Mama's advice. The fog felt clammy and dark and so were our spirits. We were all very quiet, especially Karleton. We all concentrated on finding our way to cousin Golden's apartment where we were to sleep on the floor. There was a lot to think about to get ready for our big engagement the next day. We would have to press our costumes, curl our hair, and just plain worry.

Our performance on the stage at the Gate opening day was a nightmare. We thought we knew our act well. In fact, we did but we weren't prepared for a big, movie house stage. We had been singing on the radio with a few club dates thrown in. This needed a completely different act.

Our first number was "Reflection on the Water." It was slow and beautiful and chromatic and great for harmony but no one had ever heard of it. That was our first mistake. We should have started with something fast and familiar. We then went into some of our Boswell-type numbers, "River Stay Way from My Door," "When It's Darkness on the Delta," and "Sentimental Gentleman from Georgia." Those should have been show-stoppers, but something was wrong.

Then came our big finale, "Forty-Second Street." We had a cute dance routine on this. This should have done it. Our costumes consisted of black satin skirts, slit up past our knees, white satin blouses and top hats and canes. We had seen the look on the new talkie, *Forty-Second Street,* and thought it looked sensational. We stood there in the darkened wings of the theatre, our hearts pounding, awaiting our cue. Horace had just finished announcing us and was adjusting the mike when the band played our introduction. We breathlessly ran to center stage. It seemcd quite familiar until the house lights went down, and we were standing there in utter darkness. A glaring white spot blinding us as we began singing.

Where was Maxine's lead? I couldn't hear her. Where was Alyce's low alto part? It seemed far away. I could only hear myself and my throat was dry and parched. We couldn't see anything or each other. We stumbled over our canes. I lost my hat and Horace had to recover it for me. I looked at the audience but I couldn't see anyone. All was blackness! We were accustomed to seeing people, used to seeing them smile and feel their responses.

We finally got through our act and I knew it had been a complete disaster. We rushed off the stage and didn't even take a bow. We couldn't hear the big applause we were used to and we felt wretched.

As Joe took us up the elevator, Alyce burst into tears. Naturally, Maxine and I soon joined her.

Joe said, "Hey, girls, don't feel bad. The first show is never good. Everything is new and strange. You just wait, by the last show tonight, you'll be killing them!"

I wasn't so sure about that.

Then Alyce said, "I wonder when the next bus leaves for Salt Lake."

We knew she was being sarcastic. There was no way we were going back to Salt Lake. We'd get jobs clerking at Woolworths before we did that.

Joe let us out on the third floor and we entered our dressing room. We had just started cold creaming our faces when we heard a knock at the door. What if it were Horace? We hated to face him; we had been such a flop. But there he was standing in the door with his big, wonderful, professional smile. Then he really surprised us. "Girls, you were marvelous. They loved you. We want you to stay with the band — be a permanent fixture — part of the Heidt family."

That was the first time we knew Horace had a silver tongue.

We knew we hadn't been marvelous on the stage but Horace did understand newcomers and he liked to give them a break. For this, we were thankful. But where else could he get three beautiful sisters who could sing, dance, read music, and could learn an entirely new act almost every week all for the huge salary of thirty-three and one-half dollars each per week?

That first week we literally lived on tuna fish sandwiches. Daddy and Mama had taught us not to borrow. Most acts, if they were hungry, would ask for an advance on their salaries. Not us. The thought never occurred to us so we made tuna fish sandwiches and that was our dinner each day. Mama had fed us on tuna sandwiches when we were kids doing family concerts in schools and churches. For dessert we usually had fig newtons and bananas. It was very nutritious and gave us a lot of energy. It worked for us then, why not now? That twenty-five dollars which Mama had tucked in our purses when we left Salt Lake managed to last the whole week.

Joe was right. After awhile, we got to feel right at home on stage at the Golden Gate. The spotlight didn't bother us anymore; we could see each other and we learned how to play to the audience and how to relax on stage. Horace was nice and complimented us frequently, and the boys in the band were friendly. Everyday we learned more about show business. We were beginning to feel secure.

So we rented a small one-room apartment next to the Gate and settled down to a long engagement with Horace Heidt and his big band. Since we were the family bread winners, we sent for our folks to join us in San Francisco but they decided to reside in Oakland as it was more of a "family town." They could still keep their eyes on us since San Francisco was only a ferry boat ride away.

2

The "College of Life"

Our stay at the Gate lasted almost three years. What a "college of life" for three young maidens from the provincial city on the Great Salt Lake. All our lives Daddy harped on education. Being a school teacher, one would think we could have stayed in one place. But Daddy was restless and always thought that the other pasture was greener so almost every fall we were in a different school and a different town. Ephraim, Payson, Castledale, all small Utah towns, were the settings of our early formal schooling.

A lot of our friends were going off to college despite the depression. We didn't. We couldn't afford it but we went to a better college than most of them. Backstage at the Golden Gate was our classroom and there we received an invaluable education.

First, we learned the art of make-up. There was a black wax which we heated and melted and applied to our eyelashes giving us a devastating look across the footlights. This was before false eyelashes were on the market. There were the little jars of eye shadow that accented the color of our eyes, according to which hue we applied. Then there was pancake powder that gave our skin glorious tones of suntan when the bright spotlight shone on us. We learned about the bright, shiny lipsticks that were applied with a brush. We could paint a tiny cupid's shape like Clara Bow's lips or a big, voluptuous, sexy mouth like Joan Crawford's — it was such fun — and did we experiment!

We all learned about love. Alyce, the youngest, became the first student. She fell in love with a trumpet player in the Heidt band. The trumpet player was a tall, thin, weak-looking man but he was romantic in a Leslie Howard sort of way. Evidently he had finesse and Alyce was fascinated. Until this time, Alyce had known only awkward school boys and this man was smooth and experienced and seasoned and Alyce couldn't resist him. Maxine and I worried about her. Should we tell Mama and Daddy? No, we decided. We'd better work this out ourselves. We were big girls now, out on our own.

One afternoon we found the two of them together down at Pop's Sandwich Shop. She was having a cup of coffee with him. We were shocked! Alyce knew she wasn't supposed to drink coffee and besides, we knew from the boys in the band that the trumpet player was married.

I don't know whether Maxine and I objected more to the coffee or the tete-a-tete with a married man. The sins seemed to be of equal importance to our strict Mormon up-bringing.

The next day Alyce and I were together in the dressing room. Maxine hadn't arrived.

"Alyce."

"Yes, I know — I wasn't really drinking coffee. I was just holding the cup. It seemed so corny to order hot chocolate. Nobody does that."

"I'm not talking about the coffee. I'm talking about the dreamy-eyed trumpet player."

"You don't have to call him the trumpet player. He has a name you know."

"Yes, I know. He also has a wife."

"Who told you? Jerry?"

Jerry also played trumpet in the band. His chair was next to Warren, the young man Alyce was so smitten with.

"Naturally. Jerry knows everything that's going on in the band — he's the band gossip. But I believe him. He told me about Horace and all his love affairs. Right now it's the girl harpist."

"I know. I know. Who cares? This backstage is worse than living in a small town."

"You're right, but I don't like your getting mixed up with a married man."

"I know he's married. But he's so unhappy. His wife must really be a rat if what he says is true. He's getting a divorce. He told me."

"When did he tell you that?"

"After the dance the other night. Remember, I had a date to go dancing at the Mark with Scott Lambert. Well, we went up there and who do you think was playing in the band?"

"Your trumpet player!"

"How did you know?"

"Well, Jerry told me he was playing with a dance band after his theatre job with Heidt."

"That's right and when Warren saw me, he held up his forefinger. That's how musicians get dates with girls. One finger means one o'clock, two means two, etc. I held up one finger which means that's OK. So when Scott took me home, there was Warren waiting at our apartment in his convertible, only on the other side of the street. I gave Scott a fast peck and rushed him off and got in the car with Warren. Oh, I love him so. He just has to touch my hand and I completely melt. I really think I'm in love at last."

"I'm glad because I was beginning to think you would be an old maid." Alyce wasn't seventeen yet, and I loved to be sarcastic with her about all her boyfriends. "So that's why you were out so late the other night. You had two dates in one night."

"Yes, and it was wonderful. I mean the second date. Oh,

Luise, please don't tell Mama. When Warren leaves his wife, I'll tell Mama and Daddy all about it."

"I think you're in for a lot of trouble, Alyce — I just don't know." Maxine entered the room and we dropped the subject fast. Maxine wouldn't be any more tolerant than Mama would have been.

I had cause to worry. I had been in the hall a few days before and our dressing room door was ajar. Alyce was taking a nap. Warren hadn't seen me and he entered our dressing room and bent down and kissed Alyce. She awoke and I saw the look in those blue eyes and she returned his kiss. I felt then that Alyce was really headed for trouble.

I also learned about love. After we had been with Horace about a month, a tall, shy guitarist who called himself Alvino Rey joined the band. Horace had been raving to us about this fine guitarist. He said the guitarist could stop the show cold with his sensational playing and that was pretty hard for an instrumentalist to do. It generally took a singer to sway an audience.

Horace arranged a date between Alvino and me although I wasn't sure I would like Alvino.

We were a little late getting started as we first had to do our nine o'clock show at the Gate, but we went to hear Guy Lombardo at the St. Francis Hotel. When he picked me up at our apartment next to the theatre, Alvino looked quite presentable despite his long, dark hair slicked close to his head.

"His hair is too long," I thought to myself. I preferred the short crew cuts that were popular with most of the college boys.

I was pleased with my own appearance. I was wearing a long, Jean Harlow-type, bias-cut black dress, black silk gloves that reached past my elbows and a choker string of fake pearls around my neck. Alyce told me I looked really chic.

Alvino handed me a gardenia corsage that smelled like heaven and went beautifully with my dress. "He does have good taste," I murmured.

We drove to the St. Francis in his brand new 1934 Ford

convertible. What a sporty little car! I guessed Alvino was doing all right financially since he had a job with NBC in addition to playing with Heidt.

We entered the lovely ballroom at the St. Francis where Guy Lombardo and his Royal Canadians looked resplendent in their scarlet jackets. In spite of their corny style of playing, everyone agreed it was the best dance music. Guy was great with tempos.

Of course, I wanted to dance right away. I loved to dance and had decided long ago that I would never marry anyone who couldn't dance. Dancing was my greatest enjoyment next to singing. To my dismay, Alvino said he didn't dance. He had never learned how. He had played for dances since he was a kid and had never had the chance to dance. That was my first disappointment.

We sat at a nice ringside table. I ordered a tall gingerale and Alvino said, "Make it two."

When the waiter returned with the drinks, I started sipping mine politely. Alvino sipped his too, but not before he took a small silver flask from his jacket and poured something into his gingerale. I decided he was much too sophisticated and slick for me. That was my second disappointment.

As the evening wore on, Alvino seemed to relax and be less bashful. We enjoyed the music and he even got out on the floor and walked stiffly around me, making a pretense of dancing.

After Lombardo played his good-night medley, Alvino and I headed for home in his convertible — at least I thought we were headed for home — but we were headed for the beach.

"Alvino, where are we going? I've got to get home. It's late and we have an early show tomorrow."

"I know, but I want to show you the Cliff House. My father often took my mother there for Sunday brunch. They drove in a horse and buggy, Mom with her big picture hat and white gloves and Dad in his cutaway coat, bowler and spats. They were a handsome couple. They really made the rounds of the famous San Francisco restaurants. You know they lived here before the earthquake. In fact, they were both in it."

"I think that's exciting, but can't we go there some other time? I've just got to go home."

Alvino didn't pay any attention to what I was saying. And I thought he was driving too fast. All too soon, we were there at the edge of the cliffs with the Cliff House perched over the ocean and the San Francisco fog rolling in. I shivered a little.

"I'll bet you are cold," he said as he reached over, put his arms around me, and kissed me. I should have been furious. I was, but his kiss completely melted me and I returned it with more passion that I intended.

I finally pulled myself away and said, "Alvino, please take me home."

"I will, but I want to say you're the girl I want to marry. But let's not go all the way before we're married. You are just too spiritual and sweet and I never want to spoil that quality in you."

I was flabbergasted! I should have been the one to say when to stop — not him! Here he was talking about marriage and I was thinking "I don't think I want another date with him. He's too fast and sophisticated for me."

He turned on the motor and headed for our apartment. When we arrived he stopped the car and helped me out. At his touch, I began trembling — never before had I experienced such physical passion — yet mentally, I wasn't sure I liked him at all.

But as life continued backstage at the Golden Gate, Alvino and I were thrown together daily and I began to know the real Alvino and to appreciate him as a marvelous human being. He was naturally very shy. He had spiked his drink at the St. Francis to give himself enough courage to face the evening with a girl he scarcely knew.

Our love and friendship blossomed and I found that he was not as sophisticated and slick as I had thought. He turned out to be a sweet, loving, humble, interesting, exciting, romantic, lanky tall Scotsman who only went by the name of Alvino Rey — a young man with a multi-faceted talent bordering on genius. One of his band singers, Jan Stewart, once said of him,

"If you don't like Alvino, you don't like fried chicken and apple pie." Everyone he worked with loved him and now that included me.

Between shows we would drive around the streets of San Francisco in his little convertible and Alvino would tell me of his life. I found it fascinating.

When he was eight years old and living in Piedmont, California, a radio operator visited his home to talk to his older cousin. Alvino overheard them and became intensely interested in radio. He got his mother to buy him a book entitled *How to Build a Wireless Set*. This began his building of short wave radios. His first set was a coil wound around a Quaker Oats box. He could actually pick up radio station NPG on Goat Island. Even at that tender age, he started reading everything available on radio theory and six months later decided he was ready to take an amateur test. Riding the ferry boat to San Francisco, Alvino went to the custom house at the end of Market Street. On that particular day, they were giving only commercial exams but seeing how young and determined he was, the examiners made an exception and gave him the test. They put him in a room by himself and gave him a pair of earphones. After easily passing the code, Alvino was given a list of questions and a pad of yellow paper. He wrote for two or three hours and then handed in his results. The inspector picked up his "thesis," stared at it for awhile, then gave it back saying, "I can't read a word of it. Will you please do it over?"

During his second attempt he spent more time writing legibly than expounding his knowledge and his paper was accepted. A few months later, his certificate signed by Herbert Hoover, who was then Secretary of Commerce, arrived in the mail. He assigned Alvino the call number 6 U.E. All of this happened before Alvino's ninth birthday.

When he was in his early teens, his family moved to Cleveland where one Christmas morning, his mother and father presented him with a banjo. He had asked for a saxophone, but his mother thought the mouth piece unsanitary and substituted a banjo.

Alvino had been disappointed at first, but soon became quite fascinated with his banjo and spent so much time practicing on the instrument that he practically gave up his ham radio. He became so good on the banjo that he soon was playing little dance band dates around Cleveland. When Phil Spitalny, one of the country's top band leaders, was touring the United States choosing young musicians to join his group to play in the Pennsylvania Hotel in New York City, he passed through Cleveland and auditioned young Alvin McBurney.

Alvin McBurney was Alvino's real name and he got more than the job, he got a name change. His teacher, his father, and Mr. Spitalny decided that Alvin McBurney just wouldn't do in show business so they came up with the name Alvino Rey. Both names were Spanish; *Alvino* was the Spanish form of *Alvin* and *Rey* meant *king* — appropriate considering the name of the girl he would marry.

A lot of people remember Spitalny as having the all-girl orchestra that was heard on radio in the thirties. But back in the twenties, he had an all-male orchestra that was practically the number one band in New York City. Phil Spitalny was the youngest child of a large, Russian Jewish family that settled in Cleveland. His oldest brother, Leopold, became quite famous as a contractor for NBC. Maurice, another brother, had a beautiful salon band that played in hotels in Cleveland and New York City. During their childhood, Phil, being the youngest, was expected to wait on the older brothers doing menial tasks like shining their shoes. But he managed to find time to become an accomplished musician and later formed an orchestra fine enough to play at the renowned Pennsylvania Hotel in New York.

Phil was a hard task master having been taught well by his brothers. After playing until one in the morning, he would give the musicians half an hour break for refreshment and food and then start rehearsing. This rehearsal would generally last until the sun came up and the musicians would be dismissed to go to their apartments or hotel rooms. On Sunday, their day off, they would drive up to Harlem and make records for the

Edison Recording Company and then, if they finished early enough, they would go out to Long Island or New Jersey and make film shorts to be shown between motion pictures in the theatres.

This was Alvino's introduction to playing in a big-time band. He could never complain about hard work after this experience. Phil was a slave driver who was constantly bringing musicians down by making remarks to the band members such as "You have a tone like the flushing of a toilet." It was probably Freddie Martin who was the recipient of that remark.

Naturally, Phil had a fine, well-rehearsed orchestra. He was famous for taking overtures and classics and turning them into dance band music but his band members were not too fond of Phil.

At age nineteen Alvino had not only mastered the banjo and the guitar but several other instruments and was already playing with a big-time orchestra in the world famous Pennsylvania Hotel. In that orchestra were Russ Morgan, Freddie Martin, and one of Bennie Goodman's brothers. There was a select handful of good jazz musicians in New York during that period including the Dorsey brothers, Benny Goodman, Jack Teagarden, and Eddie Lang. Alvino got to know many of these musicians by sitting in jam sessions with them. He learned to love jazz and people have always been amazed when Alvino plays at an informal jam session what good jazz he can get out of his guitar. He loved Eddie Lang's guitar playing and was greatly influenced by him. Eddie was heard on many of Bing Crosby's early recordings. When Eddie died young of a tonsillectomy, Alvino was able to purchase one of his guitars. He still has that guitar and prizes it greatly.

Alvino was in New York in 1929 during the Big Crash when Wall Street came tumbling down. He remembers some of the well-heeled customers of the Pennsylvania Hotel who jumped out of windows of hotels or office buildings or committed suicide by other means. Alvino was totally amazed that losing money would cause people to take their own lives.

Soon after the Crash, Spitalny's band broke up and Alvino and his family returned to San Francisco. He got a job on the staff at NBC as a guitar soloist. Meredith Willson was the orchestra leader at the time; Harold Peary of the "Great Gildersleeve" series was there as was "Little Orphan Annie," who, in reality, was a heavy-set woman in her forties but blessed with an adorable child-like voice. "One Man's Family," a forerunner of today's soap operas, was also a favorite Sunday afternoon show originating from NBC. The Golden Age of Radio had its beginning right there in San Francisco in the early thirties.

Not long after returning to the Bay Area, Alvino joined the Horace Heidt band and I met my dream man. He took me flying over the Golden Gate Bridge in his first little monoplane — boots, goggles, helmet, and white scarf — all the romance and adventure of "Lindy." Some of Alvino's fellow musicians called him "Ace" because of his flying expeditions. But that's another book.

He loved gourmet food and was a master chef. He could have written a book on the culinary arts. It was said that his wanting to explore the restaurants of the United States may have been his real reason for agreeing to do so many one-nighters. I suspect there is an element of truth in that.

I learned about food, and so did my sisters, thanks to Alvino, for wherever Alvino and I went, most of the time, my sisters and their boyfriends went also. They respected Alvino as a connoisseur. San Francisco was teeming with fine restaurants then as it is today and such worldly gourmet food we had never experienced. Fried chicken, mashed potatoes, and ice cream were our Utah fare. In San Francisco we experienced a whole new epicurean world. It didn't take us long to acquire a taste for bay shrimp and luscious Dungenous crab mixed in a "Luis" dressing concocted right at Henry's Fashion Restaurant on Market Street. We dined at many of the really good restaurants having such provocative names as The Poodle Dog, The Manger, The Fly Trap, The Bay City Grill, Vanessis, Bardellis, and Jack's. Many of them had private booths with curtains where you could smooch and play kneesies if you were feeling romantic with your dinner date. They were very private.

But the best part was the price. At many of the restaurants, for the sum of fifty cents, you could get celery and carrot sticks and peppers followed by a course of soup (perhaps minestrone), a shrimp or crab cocktail (fresh from the bay), a pasta (ravioli or spaghetti), a small portion of fish (probably filet of sole in wine sauce), the entree (usually lamb chops or chicken or steak), a delicious little dessert (rice pudding or banana fritters), a carafe of wine, a demi-tasse of black coffee and a loaf of sourdough bread, all of this included in the price of the dinner. It was generally prepared in French or Italian style, very hearty and delicious. Alvino loved showing us the gourmet spots of his native city.

Many times after dinner we would return to the theatre and perform what we called a dinner show feeling so stuffed we would become drowsy and even fall asleep. Horace would be furious with us and once, during a boring vaudeville act we had seen innumerable times, had pictures taken of the band and girls dozing. He warned us, "If it happens again, the whole band as well as the girls will be fired."

Looking back at it now, we are amused. I don't blame Horace. He should have fired us! Even if he had, it would have been worth it. Those glorious San Francisco dinners were something we will always remember.

We also learned about music, the music of the day. San Francisco was always known for its lovely hotels, each having bands playing for dining and dancing. They were not the big loud swing bands of Chicago and New York, but were large bands more or less geared to society-type music. We called them "Mickey Mouse" or Society bands, but they were not quite that. They were more melodic and full. At the Mark Hopkins on top of Nob Hill, Anson Weeks had everyone tapping their toes. Down at the St. Francis, Phil Harris whose band was known as Lofner and Harris, was playing in the beautiful Rose Room. Ted Fiorito generally hung out at the

St. Francis and had a beautiful little blonde girl singer, Betty Grable. The band also included Muzzy Marcellino and the Three Debutantes. Across the bay, the Tom Coakley band played at Oakland's popular Athens' Club. Tom had a handsome boy singer by the name of Eddie Howard. Eddie eventually formed his own band and was a big hit around Chicago. A society band headed by Griff Williams was playing Tate's at the Beach and was very popular with the society damsels, much like Eddie Duchin at the Plaza in New York.

What fun we had hopping around these different dance spots in the evening after our last show, gardenias pinned on our shoulders. Our escorts always sent flowers; it was part of the dating game and certainly a part of the San Francisco scene. I don't know which of the two delightful scents of San Francisco I liked best, the pungent odor of the crab pots at Fisherman's Wharf or the delicate bouquet of the gardenia corsage. After an evening of dancing, we would end up at Original Joe's for a luscious hamburger on sourdough bread with some hot Italian peppers.

Then, if that wasn't enough, we would generally park at some secluded romantic spot overlooking the bay. We wouldn't think of inviting young men to our room or going to a motel. Not us! We would sit in the car and turn the radio on, perhaps be lucky enough to get a remote and then we would neck. Sometimes pretty heavy necking if we were in love but we didn't go "all the way." I guess a lot of kids did, but we didn't. It was before the time of the pill and we knew it would be our luck to get pregnant and that was not for us! We had ambition to make something of our lives. We wanted to make our marks in the world. Perhaps the greatest deterrent was the presence of a sister along on the date; we really couldn't go very far. Also that strict Mormon training and all the standards implanted in us by our parents were always there, hanging over our heads, despite the youth and freedom and the young passion we felt and enjoyed.

So we turned the car radio on and listened to the band remotes, the Casa Loma band coming to us from the Glen

Island Casino with Kenny Sargent singing "For You" or Ben Bernie from Chicago or Guy Lombardo and his Royal Canadians from the St. Francis Hotel. We could have them all by a flip of the radio dial as we sat in Alvino's little convertible on any given foggy night as we overlooked the San Francisco Bay. We had our love to keep us warm.

Indeed, we learned about life during those years at the Golden Gate Theatre. Along with all the wonderful aspects of our lives, we also learned some difficult lessons.

We learned how Horace could take a little, untrained nobody off the streets and by presenting him to the audience in a certain way, could literally bring the house down. He had a hypnotic quality with the audience, much like Billy Graham or Oral Roberts. We also found people were swayed easily. We discovered too, that Horace could get upset with us for some innocent thing we had done and proceed to put us in the doghouse. He would not feature us for weeks and keep us in painful suspense.

We discovered that Horace was a sort of Dr. Jekyll and Mr. Hyde. When we first came with the band, he was marvelous to us. He took us to dinner at his private golf club and was thoughtful about so many things. But one time, we decided to change our hairdos and wear bangs. When he saw our hair, he sort of glared at us but said nothing. The next show we found that the songs we did on stage were cut to a bare minimum. He didn't smile at us and really gave us the cold shoulder. What had we done to make him so disenchanted?

We worried and fretted and lost our appetites. Later, we learned that he objected to the bangs and when we went back to our old hairdos, he was nice and friendly again and our songs came back on the program.

Being at the Golden Gate Theatre for over three years was like living in a small, gossipy town. Everyone knew everything that was going on as the boys in the band were adept at passing on tales. We learned that Horace was married to a lovely society lady. We also heard he didn't have too much of a marital relationship with her because of his "back injuries."

(That's what he told her). We also heard that he was carrying on with the voluptuous, young harpist in the band. That was easy to believe when we saw the subtle looks pass between them.

We also found that Horace was a slave driver. We rehearsed and rehearsed between shows. We griped and hated him most of the time. But it paid off. The Alemite Company of Chicago wanted to sponsor the band on the radio as well as having us play at the plush Drake Hotel on the Gold Coast. We were thrilled with thoughts of going back to that big city; all the big bands were playing there. Of course our folks weren't too excited about it. They were worried about us and hated to see their daughters go so far away. We had appeared on the front page of the *San Francisco Examiner* dressed as three little bar maids. Our folks were furious when they saw the picture of their three little Mormon girls blowing foam off mugs of beer. We hadn't given it a thought. We were thrilled to have our picture on the front page of the *Examiner.* It was part of a publicity stunt to celebrate the end of Prohibition and "happy days" and Roosevelt were here to stay. We were happy about it, too. Eleanor and Franklin liked show folks and show business.

We were all looking forward to a huge success with Horace Heidt and his band in the big city of Chicago. We had started out as a trio but now there would be four of us.

During our stay at the Gate, Maxine had married her hometown sweetheart, LaVarn Thomas. He had left Salt Lake and come to San Francisco to get a job in order to be close to Maxine. He had thought about joining the Heidt Glee Club but decided against it. Although he was a good singer, he felt show business was an unsure way to make a living.

Maxine's heart was never in show business and she knew she had two younger sisters who were dying to take her place. Donna was next in line so we decided to give her an opportunity by taking her to Chicago with us, knowing that Maxine would soon be leaving.If Horace would let us sing four-part harmony, maybe Yvonne could join us after Maxine left.

Horace wasn't crazy about four-part harmony. He said it sounded too far out and people wouldn't understand it. But we loved it, and we wanted to be the first female group to do it. The Merry Macs, a brother act that was causing a stir in the musical world, had been singing four-part and we loved their style, so we asked Horace if we could be a quartet instead of a trio.

When he met our cute, plump, friendly, little sister, he couldn't resist her. "Well, if I can get the four of you for the same price as three, it's a deal. Donna can sit on the piano bench and turn music for Gene Knotts, our pianist, and we can use her in finales and choral music with the glee club."

We had other ideas, although we didn't tell Horace at the time. We were anxious to have Donna at any price. Horace was happy. Four girls for the price of three, he didn't mind at all.

3

Chicago

When we arrived in Chicago in the mid-thirties, we found it to be a bustling, lively city filled with excitement and glamour. We had heard a lot about it and the thing we remembered most was "gangsters." We had seen them in the movies. We had watched Edward G. Robinson, dynamic and single-purposed; James Cagney, jaunty and with a sense of humor even in his most murderous role; and "Bogey," callous, a cold-blooded cynicism. In the pictures we saw, they portrayed the kingpins of gangdom leading lives of violence and terror and of wealth and glamour.

But we really didn't have to worry about any of that; Prohibition had been repealed. Of course, Prohibition hadn't affected our family. We were Mormons and everyone knew we had a strict code about drinking. However, there were some old Danish families back in Ephraim, Utah, who made their own home brew and we had been warned to stay away from them. Now, all we had to worry about was how well we could sing and how great the band was. We were anxious to show off for our Windy City friends and all those big bands!

Nearly every big band was in Chicago. The Congress Hotel, with its revolving stage, was featuring Benny Goodman who had just come from the Palomar Ballroom in Los Angeles. He had a slinky, sexy girl singer by the name of Helen Ward. She had a subtle way of moving her hips that really fascinated the public — plus, she was a good singer. When she warbled, "Goody, Goody," the crowd went wild. Of course, they watched more than Helen. A handsome kid named Gene Krupa was a show himself when he beat on his drums. At the piano was Jess Stacy, a great artist Benny had picked up in Denver. A little later, Teddy Wilson was to join the band and then there was Bunny Berigan blowing his soul out in the brass section. Certainly the biggest attraction was Benny himself. He didn't get the title of "King of Swing" for nothing. He was and still is the master of his instrument. Benny's band really started the swing era.

Also in the Windy City was the fabulous Casa Loma Band with the elegant Glen Grey fronting it. The band looked stunning in their white ties and tails, and the college kids adored them.

It was in Chicago that we met Ozzie Nelson and Harriet Hilliard. Ozzie was fronting his band at the Palmer House and Harriet was hopping back and forth from the coast with a new picture contract. How we marvelled at her beautiful grooming and lovely clothes. She taught us a lot of trade beauty secrets: how to apply false eyelashes so that they really looked natural and how to use a lipstick brush to give a clean-cut, natural look to the lips. We have enjoyed the friendship of the Nelsons, a beautiful lady and a wonderful couple, for many years.

There wasn't a hotel of any size that didn't have a band: the Panther Room at the Sherman, the Congress Hotel, the Stevens, the Drake and many more.

The Drake Hotel on the plush Gold Coast was to be the home of Horace Heidt and his band for the next few years.

When we arrived at the Silver Forest in the hotel, it was a mad house. Busboys and waiters were busily setting up tables and countless workers on ladders and tables were tying silver leaves to the ceiling. It looked a little like a high school prom in the stark light of the afternoon, but when we saw it at night for the first time, it proved to be quite effective theatrically. We had never performed at a plush hotel and the afternoon of the opening night, we thought we would never make it. We were still rehearsing at five-thirty and the dining room was a cluttered mess.

But by 7:00 p.m., the enchanting Silver Forest and the enthusiastic King Sisters were ready. Ben Marshal, manager of the Drake Hotel, had designed our dresses which were made of gold material appearing more like paper than cloth. He was sort of a lecherous, little, old, very artistic man with longish hair and a goatee. He always wore a flowing windsor tie. He had his hands in everything —from the apple pie he created for the dining room (he told us that he always left the peelings on the apples to give it a magnificent flavor) — to the gowns for the performers. The gowns he designed for us were stunning, but fragile.

About midnight, when one of the dancing customers, a little inebriated by champagne, tugged at sister Donna's skirt to request a song, the skirt pulled completely off, revealing the two dimpled knees of our plump, little sister. In unison we shrieked and retired to the dressing room. Naturally, when something happened to one of our dresses, we all had to change costumes but we wondered what our conservative parents would have said about this turn of events. Mr. Marshal would just have to stick to creating apple pies and let us do our own costume designing—which he did from that day on.

We had been in Chicago for a short time when I decided I should write to Mama and Daddy. I knew Mama wouldn't feel too useful for awhile with only three children at home; the house would seem empty and forlorn to her. We had lived in our own apartment in San Francisco but we would always rush over to Oakland on our day off and we weren't so far away that Mama would feel sad. But it was a long way to Chicago and I could see Mama going out to the mailbox, scanning through the bills and advertisements, looking for a letter from her girls.

We had been terribly busy, but that really was no excuse.

May 18, 1935

Dear Mama and Daddy,

At last we're in Chicago and what a thrill it is. We are staying at the Knickerbocker Hotel across the street from the Drake Hotel where we will be singing We can almost hop out of bed onto the bandstand. We're also just a block from Lake Michigan and it's very beautiful and swanky. They call it the "Gold Coast." But before I tell you more about Chicago, let me describe our first cross-country trip on the big charter bus.

Maybe we didn't cry as much as you did, Mama, when we left you, but as soon as that bus started moving, it suddenly dawned on us — we're really leaving home — and it was very quiet for awhile. I think each one of us had hidden our tears and now our muffled sobs could be detected all over the bus. Perhaps, never again would we really live at home with you. It was a realization none of us had contemplated in our excitement of packing and leaving for Chicago. Suddenly, our sincere desire to be famous and grown-up seemed to be the farthest thing from our minds.

We remember what you said, Mama, about keeping an eye on one another, so we sat up front just behind Horace, like good little girls. But wouldn't you know it, Alyce heard some of the fellows in the back laugh, and she managed to wind her way to the rear of the bus, where a hot poker game was in session. She claimed she was only watching, but with those flirting, big eyes she was quite a distraction. Mama and Daddy, I don't want to be telling on Alyce, but I know she likes one of the trumpet players and he's married. But she thinks it's all right because he told Alyce he's leaving his wife. He claims she doesn't understand him.

By the way, Vonnie looked so little and lost when we left for Chicago, standing there waving as the bus rolled away. I hope she isn't too hurt because Horace said he couldn't afford five of us. Actually, the four of us are working for the price of three. We have an idea about singing four-part harmony, but I don't think Horace will like it. It's a little far out for him. But we are still going to try it. We would be the first female group to do this.

In the meantime, Donna sits on the piano bench and turns the music for the piano player. She also spends a lot of time down at the tables, entertaining the plush customers. She is so sweet and friendly.

But back to the trip. We loved it, although it was a far cry from our old Dodge touring car that took us on all those trips together.

Our first one-nighter was in Reno and we stayed in the Riverside Hotel, the best in the city, so we felt pretty deluxe! After the show and broadcast, I had a date with Alvino, Alyce went out with the trumpet player, and Maxine stayed in her room and wrote her love. That left Donna sort of on her own. The boys in the glee club invited her out to see the town, you know, just walk around and see all the bright lights. She saw the bright lights, all right. They wandered into a red light district and the ladies in their kimonos all started yelling and calling to the boys and waving to them. They didn't seem to like the idea of the boys bringing a girl along. Naturally, they weren't going up to the girls' rooms; they were just walking along the street. We didn't even know what a red light district was until the boys explained it to us. Mama and Daddy, this will never happen again. We will promise to stick together just like you told us to and we will always remember whose daughters we are. The girls all send their love.

Your loving daughter,

Luise

After I sent that letter, we received a letter back from Daddy, as fast as the airmail could fly it back to Chicago.

May 21, 1935

My Darling Daughters,

When we received Luise's letter from Chicago and finished reading it, Mama's face went white as a sheet. She said, "King, I think we made a mistake letting the girls go out on their own so young." I told her that it was life and you girls were going to learn about it sooner or later. We have given you a good foundation and you are not going to falter. We will all trust in the Lord.

We don't have to tell you how happy we were to receive your long looked-for letter, even tho it did upset us. We are glad you have arrived safely at your destination. I'm sure you will find Chicago an exciting place to be, as your Mother and I did many years ago.

Need I say that it's been a lonesome, old house since your departure. The fact that we lost Karleton at the same time didn't help matters any. As you know, since he was not needed to accompany you any longer, the offer to play on the *Dollar Liner* was well-timed. He will be able to keep his hand in music and see the world besides. How I envy him, but this adventure is well-earned by our faithful Karleton whose only thought has always been for the family.

And now my dear Maxine, named after the great Maxine Elliot, I know you are lonely for your LaVarn, but your decision to have a glimpse of life before you settle down to being a wife and mother was a good one. So when you want to come back (you have always said that show business doesn't hold much glamour for you) just say the word and Yvonne will be more than ready to step into your shoes. If anyone was ever cut out for show business, she is! We'll even drive her back in Put-Put — that will be a good excuse to see our girls.

Luise, my grey-eyed Athene, Goddess of Wisdom, you have always had such a good head on your shoulders, I do not fear for you. Alvino is such a fine chap. I know you will be able to work and live together in harmony when the proper time comes.

Alyce, my little Theda Bara vamp, I am deeply concerned about you. God has endowed you with a beautiful voice, large expressive eyes and seductive ways. You will always have men clamoring for your attention. But your price must be high and you must wait for a virtuous young man who can give you cleanness of body and spirit. With your talent and beauty, you will have many temptations. But if you are virtuous, you will be rewarded with a long and lasting love.

Donna Olivia, named after your beloved grandmother, you are so very young and trusting, with your sociability and friendly ways. People will always love you, but you must be cautious. The older girls have given us their word that they will look after you, and so it will be.

From now on, I am going to be very busy. I have a new position working for the W.P.A. I am leading a chorus and will be giving a monthly concert at the Oakland Civic Auditorium. I am busy composing a cantata which I plan to present in the spring.

I said I am going to trust in the Lord, but in case he needs some help, I am enclosing a theology lesson, which I have written for you. I just read it to Mama and she said it was too deep, the sentences were too long and ambiguous and too involved. She also said that I was just trying to show off my prolific knowledge and superfluous vocabulary. I guess she is right, but I am sending it to you for what it is worth, hoping that you may gain a few thoughts from it, and that it may serve as a little spiritual food during this time of your spiritual famine, isolated as you are from all religious contacts.

I am so creative, I just have to be creating something all the time or I am not happy. My thoughts sound so wonderful to my mental ear while I am writing them, but when I read them aloud, they are not so hot. At least the wording in which they are clothed is punk. Most of the output of my original mind, in fact, about 999 specimens out of 1,000 of my writings, paintings and composing turn out that way, "ain't worth a damn." But 1 out of 1,000 turns out OK. I guess I ought to be satisfied as long as I get joy out of the process. So read it over and if you "no savvy," just take the will for the deed and know that I am trying to help you a little in this way if I can't in any other.

Say your prayers and don't forget whose daughters you are and all will be well with you. May God bless you.

Love,

Dear Daddy Driggs

Maxine said the word and before we knew it, Mama and Daddy had arrived in Chicago by way of Put-Put, with fourteen-year-old Yvonne. The world was Yvonne's oyster.

She walked into the Silver Forest of the Drake Hotel, looked up at the cut-out leaves on the ceiling and said, "This looks like the ceiling of a high school gymnasium at a senior prom."

Horace gave her a double-take and I could tell what he was thinking. He wasn't sure he would be so happy with this little outspoken woman-child who was taking Maxine's place. Yvonne was not all sweetness and goodness like Maxine, and she could be a problem to Horace but she was a firecracker and cute as a pistol. She gave our sister act a much-needed zing and we were happy she came.

Maxine left the group and went home to her sweet husband, LaVarn but she left the King Sisters something more important than her voice. She designed and made all our gowns for years to come. Maxine was a perfectionist; we learned that "the needle" was her real talent.

We loved pretty clothes, and felt that a lot of girl singers in the bands didn't dress up enough. But we knew if we were going to be something in our career, we must also look like something. So we frequented the more expensive dress salons in the department stores and asked to see their most stunning creations. Vonnie, the artist of the group, would take out her pencil and sketch. Then we would go home and add our two-cents worth. The skirts should be full to cover our ample hips, the waists should be tight to show off our small waists, the necks should be a little low to show off our well-endowed bosoms, but not too low, because Mama and Daddy would not stand for that.

We then went to the yardage section and bought yards and yards of satin, velvet and chiffon. If we wanted roses on the material, we would stretch the yardage down the hall of the hotel and Vonnie would hand paint them on. Then we would send the material to Maxine with our measurements and designs, and she would create four gowns for us. Maxine became so adept at sewing that we later opened a dress shop in the San Fernando Valley, and Maxine designed clothes for a lot of movie stars.

One afternoon she was doing a dress for Jane Russell and

was called to the phone. Jane was standing on a table in all her glorious nudity and Maxine's husband, LaVarn, innocently walked in on Jane. His face blushed a fire-engine red, and he ran out of the house slamming the door. He had seen Jane without her famous bra that had been designed especially for her by Howard Hughes.

Shortly after we opened at the Drake, I noticed that Alyce was getting awfully thin and her voice started getting husky. One night she couldn't get even one note out. She explained that it was probably the air conditioning in the hotel. It was the first time we had been in air conditioning, but I had reasons to believe it was something else, so I decided to find out what was going on.

We were getting undressed for bed. It was about two o'clock in the morning.

"Alyce, you're getting thin. You're much thinner than I and we've always weighed the same. You don't look or sound good at all. You've always told me I was your closest sister, how come you haven't confided in me?" I had noticed she was going straight to bed after the job and not going out to eat with her trumpet player. "I never see you with Warren anymore."

"And you won't see me with him anymore. He's married, you know, very much so." Her eyes started filling with tears.

"I know he's married, but you told me he was going to leave his wife." It upset me to see Alyce cry.

"Well, he's not. He lied to me. She's back here in Chicago and they're living together happy as two turtle doves. I was walking down the hall on the second floor of our hotel, a door was open and there was Warren and his wife standing there as big as life and he had his arms around her."

"Oh, how terrible for you."

"Yes, it was sickening, but I decided to get the story straight once and for all. I walked right in on them!"

"How did you have enough nerve?"

"I don't know, I just had to. I said, 'Warren, is this your wife?' He flushed and looked embarrassed and said, 'Doris, I want you to meet Alyce King of the King Sisters.' Then I said,

'I've heard so much about you through Warren.' Then I really got up my nerve. 'But I heard that you were separated and planning a divorce.' She said, 'Wherever did you get that idea? I'm telling you, the way this band gossips, you can't believe a word they say. We are very happy, and have always been. We wouldn't think of getting a divorce. Isn't that true, Warren?' She looked at Warren and he still looked embarrassed. I looked straight at Warren, right in his pale blue eyes, those dreamy eyes that I had been so attracted to, but now they were having trouble holding their gaze. 'Yes, that's true,' he said and then looked over at Doris with a half-hearted sickening smile. I ran out of the room and climbed up three sets of back stairs to get to our room. I didn't want to throw up in the elevator! I haven't seen him alone since and I don't intend to. Believe me, this is the only time I will ever have anything to do with a married man, you can be sure of that."

I put my arms around her and she sobbed her heart out. How unthoughtful I had been with my closest sister. I had been so wrapped up with my own love for Alvino, I hadn't even noticed what was going on around me.

Before Daddy and Mama left for home in Put-Put, he gathered his daughters around him and held a family meeting.

"Girls, Mama and I are proud of you. We are proud of our beautiful daughters, the way you look and the way you sing and the customers there at the Drake have gone out of their way to tell us what lovely girls you are. But there's one thing we are not proud of. You are not going to church like we have taught you to do and that makes us very sad. What are we going to do about that?"

We all mumbled excuses about how late we worked, how far the church was, how we had no transportation except a streetcar, how we had to transfer several times to get to the church.

Daddy and Mama were not impressed with our excuses. They were both from pioneer families who had crossed the plains against all odds. Mama's father had even pushed his crippled father all the way to Utah in a handcart. Our excuses seemed flimsy to them.

"I am anxious to get back to California to start my W.P.A. job, but we will wait until Sunday and see that you get to Church and are properly introduced."

Sunday morning dawned and we were a little late arising. We told Mama and Daddy to go ahead and we would meet them at Sunday School. When Sunday School started and we hadn't shown up, Daddy was furious. When they were singing the closing hymn, in dragged their four lovely daughters and sat on the back row. After the meeting, we saw Daddy go to the Bishop and talk to him. He escorted the Bishop to the back row and introduced us.

"Your father," said the bishop, "has requested that we hold a special Sunday School session for you and we've decided to do it. You just sit right here where you are and I'll go get the Sunday School teacher, a deacon, and the choir leader. Might as well do it up right for such special young ladies."

Daddy was a determined man who taught his lesson well, a lesson we were not soon to forget. After that, on Sunday morning, we set the alarm an hour ahead.

We enjoyed sitting on the bandstand each evening watching the handsomely attired people in tails and evening gowns dining and dancing. We thought they must be terribly rich to afford such an elegant place nightly. And most of the customers did come back often. There was a homey feeling about Heidt's band and he attracted people of quality rather than the typical cafe-society type. Heidt's clientele consisted primarily of wealthy business executives and their wives and families. Horace was manly, handsome, and had an athletic wholesomeness that the public seemed to like. They also seemed to find us quite appealing. Many would come back time and time again and bring their whole families. Before long, we got to know a lot of people on rather intimate terms. They called us their "Heidt Family." Many beautiful and lasting friendships began right there at the Drake.

We table-hopped between dance sets. Heidt encouraged it and the patrons loved it. It was funny to us that these heads of big companies, New York Central Railroad, Coca Cola,

Baldwin Locomotive, Stewart Warner, and Zenith Radio, enjoyed conversing with, as we perceived ourselves, four little Mormon girls. They didn't try to make passes. They were there with their wives and families and treated us like their daughters.

As I look back at our Chicago scene now, we had a front row center seat on "life and the world." But how different our lives were from that described by Doris Day when she reminisced about her sordid band life on the road. We were young, beautiful and voluptuous, with all the curves of Grable and Turner. Why we were treated with such respect I'll never quite understand. Probably having a sister looking over the shoulder helped.

One night, a tall, dark, burly man with an ugly glare on his face, walked up to the bandstand and pulled determinedly at Horace's coattails. Horace leaned down to hear him, but it was unnecessary as he boomed out in a deep, bass voice, "Horse's Hide, I like Keeng Seesters. I want Keeng Seesters come down my table. Buy drink. Meet my friends."

"The King Sisters are going to sing the next chorus," Horace told him. "But I'll tell you what. Donna isn't singing in this number. She can visit with you at your table if she'd like."

Donna looked at us hesitatingly. "We promised Daddy to keep an eye on her and all stick together," I was thinking. But I said, "Go ahead, Donna, it's all right. We'll join you at his table just as soon as this dance set is over."

With his surly face turning to a grin, he grabbed and pulled her off the bandstand and she followed, trembling, believing with all her heart that she was going to meet her doom at the hands of this Chicago gangster.

At the end of the set, we rushed to the table to rescue Donna. Imagine our surprise when we found her devouring a mammoth dish of Baked Alaska.

"Sit down, girls," she giggled happily. There are plates for all of you, so come have some."

As the man made room for us at the table, he said, "Donna told us you Keeng Seesters didn't drink so we ordered something more to your liking. You like ice cream, no?" He smiled and suddenly looked so kind we sat down with relief and attacked our Baked Alaska unafraid.

We learned he was not a Chicago gangster, but an executive with the Kimberly-Clark Paper Company. He became a good friend of ours, and the only bad thing he ever did was to make us gain a few pounds as night after night, he would come to the Drake and lavish Cherries Jubilee or Baked Alaska on us.

There were other friendships made while at the Drake that had great influence on our lives but were not so fattening. Hobnobbing with these fancy folks taught us a lot about social graces, but there were a few shins kicked under the table when one of us said the wrong thing. Yvonne, the baby, the one who was so outspoken and frank, was especially prone to putting her foot in her mouth. One evening we were sitting at a table with the president of Coca Cola. When asked to have a drink, Vonnie gaily quipped, "You're not going to drink any more of those Cokes, are you? They're worse than liquor!" He laughed and ordered lemonade.

It may sound as though we were prissy young ladies, but we really were not. We were friends and pals to the boys in the band. We loved their humor and their craziness and were crazy right along with them, always ready for a prank or a good joke. Some of the happiest hours of our lives were spent in the back dressing rooms of hotels and ballrooms, talking, laughing, and plotting jokes to be played on one another. We worked hard at the Drake, Horace saw to that, but we played just as hard. We were always anxious to see and visit with all the bands that were in town.

Ted Fiorito's band, fresh from California, was out at the Edgewater Beach Hotel where we would spend a lot of time "wrapping" with Muzzy and the Three Debutantes. Earl "Father" Hines had started another season at the Grand Terrace Cafe. Sunday night was our night off and we would go there and "dig" those big, wonderful Black Reviews. Sometimes we would be among the few white people (mostly musicians) in the audience. We were treated well and did not fear any racial disputes. We had respect for their music and they did ours. Later we could take a cab down to the Alabam Barbecue on Lake Street for barbecue ribs whose spicy flavoring made my mouth blister. These were the best ribs I've tasted.

A few years ago on one of our trips to Chicago, we started reminiscing about the Alabam Barbecue. We began thinking about the divine flavor of those ribs and asked a cab to take us there. There was no way that the driver was going to take us to that part of town; he thought it much too dangerous for him and for us. Change, I suppose, is inevitable.

We enjoyed hearing Art Tatum at the Three Dances. We struck up a friendship with him that lasted until his death in the fifties. Later when we lived in California again, Art came often to brother-in-law Buddy Cole's house. We would barbecue a leg of pork for him. He said he didn't want to fool around with just ribs; they were much too dainty!

A young Italian singer, Perry Como, was being featured with the Ted Weems band, along with Elmo Tanner, Country Washburn, and Red Ingles. All were appearing at the Trianon Ballroom. If anyone cared to waltz, Wayne King was playing it sweetly at the Aragon Ballroom. Buddy Rogers, blowing every instrument in the band, was jumping all over the bandstand at the College Inn of the Sherman Hotel. Back in the twenties, he had appeared at the Chicago Theatre, and told us a funny story about meeting Al Capone at that time.

Buddy was a movie star who every mother's daughter (including us) adored. However, at one point he found his career sagging and could not understand why. He was a great lover of music and was a musician of sorts, playing a little at each horn. He suggested to his Hollywood studio that it would be helpful to his career to front a band and travel around the country. They agreed, and he played at various big hotels and theatres.

One night the theatre manager in Chicago told him that Al Capone had requested Buddy to come to his apartment for dinner. Buddy's mother, "Mama Rogers," was traveling with him at the time, so she went along with Buddy, although they were both a little nervous about the invitation. The manager assured them there was no danger involved and escorted them to Al's apartment. When they entered Capone's apartment, on either side of the door were "hoods," with hats pulled down over their eyes, reading newspapers, just like in the movies.

Inside the lavish apartment was Al Capone himself, graciously inviting Buddy and his mother to join him for the spaghetti dinner on the table. The food was superb; the conversation was directed by Al. "Isn't it terrible all the violence that is being portrayed these days in the movie houses?"

And Al never left the subject. They finished their meal, and Buddy and his mother hurried back to the theatre to do the last show. Handsome, sweet Buddy Rogers, a "mother's darling." Why had Al Capone invited him to dinner? Was Buddy his movie idol? Buddy said he never learned the answer.

One of our favorite places to go on Monday night was the Black Hawk where Joe Sanders, the "ole left-hander," was a big attraction. He had a trumpet player, Jack Cathcart, who was dating Alyce. Some years later, Jack married one of the Gumm sisters. He helped another of those sisters, Judy Garland, in her rise to stardom. But at this time, Jack was pretty smitten with Alyce, and Alyce seemed to have a fondness for trumpet players.

One night a week, the Black Hawk held a sort of professional Amateur Night, and because it was the "dark night" for most performing people, they came in droves just to be with one another and perhaps, be in on the discovery of some new talent. One night when the four of us were in the audience, three sisters, fresh from Minneapolis, were introduced and sang with great showmanship and appeal. We enjoyed them that night, but didn't really pay any more attention to them until two or three years later, when a new record broke out on the air waves like gangbusters, "Bie Mir Bist du Schaen," and the Andrews Sisters became the number one girl trio for many years to come.

Not long after our introduction to the Andrews Sisters, we

also met Mel Torme for the first time. We marveled at the talent of the little kid drummer playing with the great Chico Marx Band.

There was a lot of hero worshipping among the sidemen of the big bands as well. *Down Beat* and *Metronome* and other music magazines made them almost as famous as their leaders. After all, Krupa was playing drums for Goodman, and it was a toss-up which people came to hear — Benny on the clarinet or Gene on the drums — or if that wasn't to one's liking, Harry James on the trumpet or Teddy Wilson on the piano were just as fascinating. The list was long in all the bands, famous then and now. They were all a part of the Chicago band scene of the thirties.

We were a part of that big band scene. Four Mormon girls from Utah, whose father had taught them to love music, still had each other to create and share the excitement, glamour and hard work of the big bands. Everyday we mingled with many of the musicians who were making Chicago such a big band attraction.

We not only worked on the Gold Coast, we lived there. We enjoyed living in the Knickerbocker Hotel which was across the street from the Drake. We heard it had been the home of Al Capone. He had occupied the entire top floor before he was arrested for tax evasion and now he had a home which wasn't so luxurious.

The Knickerbocker was modern and inexpensive and convenient and a lot of musicians lived there so it was natural to become acquainted as we met in the coffee shops and restaurants around the neighborhood.

The Knickerbocker Hotel was our home for the three years we stayed in Chicago. We loved our lives in the Windy City but the curtain was ready for us in New York City.

New York

The scene in Europe was quite confusing. The Popular Front, the leftist party in France, the German Socialist Democrats, and the Communist Party in Moscow were all fighting the capitalist system, but at the same time, fighting among themselves. A few intellects, along with Daddy, believed the European situation was building to what would become the great world war.

In America, most of the people were too busy pulling themselves out of the Great Depression to think about Europe and its problems. The rich were still hating Roosevelt; we heard them talking about him constantly at the Drake Hotel in Chicago. The poor were still loving him. We did, too, for personal reasons. Daddy lead an orchestra and chorus in the W.P.A. program.

Most of the rich kids from Harvard, Yale, Princeton, Wellesley, and Smith were concerned about getting to New York for the weekend and having fun on the town. The biggest worry of the college boys was getting a date to dance to the big bands. They all met "under the clock" at the Biltmore, their popular front.

After a three-year stint in Chicago, Horace Heidt and his Brigadeers finally made it to the big city of New York. Bands, like other theatrical performers, found it necessary to have the Big Apple label on them before they were considered important. Thus, all bands tried very hard to get booked in New York.

Heidt's band was engaged to open at the Bowman Room at the Biltmore Hotel, a hangout for college kids. Boys from Harvard, Yale and other ivy league colleges met regularly "under the clock." To us they looked smooth with their crew cuts, their pants ending two inches above saddle oxfords, their button-down collars and Brooks Brothers suits. The girls they met were smooth, too. Shiny, bobbed hair, creamy complexions, well-tailored cloth coats trimmed in mink and fox gave them an air of sophistication. The girls seemed very sure of themselves as they lit their cigarettes and downed their scotch and soda and rye high balls.

We had never heard of these concoctions and decided to try some. It was such terrible tasting stuff, we decided to stick with lemonade!

We did enjoy watching the kids come to the Biltmore to dance. They danced the Big Apple and the Shag. Jitterbugging had not quite reached its peak; the music of the thirties was too smooth for it. And what beautiful music it was! Great show tunes and magnificent melodies and lyrics, written by the master tunesmiths: Cole Porter, Irving Berlin, Noel Coward, Mack Gordon, Arthur Freed, Ray Noble, Jimmy McHugh, Richard Rogers, Gus Kahn, George Gershwin. The list goes on and on. The songs — "Night and Day," "I'm in the Mood for Love," "Red Sails in the Sunset," "Stairway to the Stars," "These Foolish Things," "When I Grow Too Old to Dream," "I Get a Kick Out of You" — will never be surpassed.

It was at the Biltmore that we first met the song publishers or song-pluggers, as we called them. They came in nightly to sell their songs. They wined and dined us and would do almost anything to get us to plug their tunes on the air. If we wanted to see a New York show, they would get us tickets. If we wanted to buy jewelry, they could get it wholesale. Most of the song pushers were Jewish and knew their music in addition to knowing what was going on in show business. Larry Shane, Herb Monte, Sidney Mills, Sam Weiss, Jack Bregman, Milt Samuels, and Mickey Goldsen were among the countless song publishers we met. Some we loved a lot, and some not so much. They were a big part of the band business and could make a band by giving it a hit tune.

While playing the Biltmore, Horace introduced a contest that was very popular with the public. It was called "Can You Pick a Star?" One night a talented, seventeen-year-old lad won the contest. He was marvelous at imitations. He did Eleanor and Franklin Roosevelt to perfection. Little did we realize that night that Art Carney would become a super star. It was Heidt who discovered him and gave him his start.

Our friend Ozzie Nelson had just arrived in New York, and with his band was playing at the Lexington Hotel. Guy Lombardo was at the Roosevelt. Benny Goodman was at the Pennsylvania, Jimmie Dorsey at the New Yorker and Tommy Dorsey was holding forth at the Commodore. Skeets Herfurt was playing sax with Tommy, and Axel Stordahl and Paul Weston arranged some of the Dorsey hits such as "Marie" and "Dream." Our good friend, Jack Egan, who had done publicity for the Ozzie Nelson band in Chicago was now doing publicity for Tommy's band. All these friends were in New York with us. We picnicked, we played tennis or golf in the afternoons and after our dance job was through, we frequented the swinging little jazz joints on Fifty-second Street until the wee, small hours. At the Onyx Club, the Hickory House, or the Famous Door, we heard Art Tatum, Maxine Sullivan or Stuff Smith. All of these were jazz greats and we had the pleasure of knowing them.

Through Jack Egan we became quite good friends with Tommy Dorsey. He invited us out to Bernardsville, his beautiful New Jersey country home, presided over by his sweet wife, Toots. There was a rumor that they were having marital troubles, and I suppose it was true because she left him shortly after that. There were stories going around the band about Edith Wright and Tommy. Often there was something going on between the girl singer and the orchestra leader. Most leaders' wives led a pretty dull existence with their husbands working every night of the week, often on the road. And there was always the young female public that went wild over musicians and band leaders. Female fans were forever throwing themselves at the feet of the band leader just as they do celebrities of today. The show business atmosphere, in general, was not conducive to good marriages.

Between wives, Tommy dated Alyce a few times but Alyce was a more experienced young lady now and knew how to handle aggressive band leaders and musicians and still remain good friends with them. I'll never know how she accomplished this since I had no problems with musicians. I was deeply in love with Alvino.

In May of 1937, after a five-year courtship, Alvino and I decided to get married. The reason — we had two weeks off — our first real vacation since we met at the Golden Gate Theatre in San Francisco. The band was also excited about this long-awaited vacation. All of us were down at the little drugstore in Grand Central Station, the snack bar closest to the Biltmore. We had an intermission from nine to ten o'clock each evening.

"Where do you think you'll go on your vacation?" Alyce was sipping hot chocolate with Jerry Bowne, the friendly little trumpet player with Heidt, the one who had warned her about Warren.

"We're going to Bermuda. What a spot! Say, you sisters should go there. It's beautiful. You'd love it," Jerry responded.

Yvonne and Donna and some of the boys in the band were huddled around, sharing vacation plans.

"I think it would be wonderful. We've never been any place off the East Coast," Vonnie said. "Luise, don't you think that would be glorious?"

I looked at Alvino and he looked at me.

"Yeah, that would be great, I suppose," he said quietly.

Donna said, "Can you believe the tans we'd come back with?"

"I haven't had any real sun since we left California."

I could tell Alyce was visualizing herself in that pale pink accordian-pleated skirt and low-cut linen halter. She would look devastating in it with a golden tan on her back.

Later that evening, Alvino cornered me alone.

"Where do you want to go on vacation, Luise? It looks like the whole band is going to Bermuda."

"Well, that's one place I don't want to go. I'm sick of beir g with the whole band!" I meant it.

"Let's get married. We've waited long enough. Let's just get in my convertible and head down the coast towards Virginia Beach. We'll stop on the way and 'tie the knot' with some local judge."

Alvino was now the proud owner of a paıe green Packard convertible that had red leather seats. He hadn't had much chance to use it during our New York stay.

I looked up at Alvino. I loved him so. I didn't need the band or my sisters or my religion or even my parents. I wanted Alvino and that's all I could think of.

"Why not? I think it would be fun. We won't make any big wedding plans. We'll just go off together and get married quietly."

Alvino reached down to me and gave me a sweet, tender kiss and rushed back to the bandstand where the band was well into their first number.

I felt good. I knew I had said the right thing to him.

We did a few one-nighters before the band was to leave on vacation. The last appearance was in Buffalo, New York, and Alvino and I got our marriage license there in the city hall.

We were playing Shea's Buffalo Theatre the night before the vacation began — the night before my wedding day. I was feeling low, suffering from a real case of the blues. We were planning to take the train back to New York that night and I was standing by the stage door with my bags. Larry Cotton, one of Heidt's singers, came up to me and put his arms around me.

"Luise, you don't look very happy and you should be on cloud nine. Aren't you getting married tomorrow?"

"Yes," I replied, "but for some reason I feel sad and lonely. I miss my mom and dad, I miss my family, I miss my sisters, even the boys in the band. They should be at my wedding and no one's going to be there except Alvino and me."

Larry pulled out a big fistful of quarters. "Luise, I'm going to give you a little wedding present. I have all these quarters, there's a pay phone right here and you're going to use them to call your mom and dad."

We did, and it was so reassuring to me to hear their dear voices. They felt terrible that they couldn't be at my wedding. We hadn't given them time enough to make plans. Karleton was getting married also, and they were planning a big wedding for him. They just couldn't be in two places at once. I was happy for Karleton. He had found himself a sweet girl and deserved his happiness. I hung up and felt a little better.

Larry had some more ideas. "You know I'm living in that beautiful apartment with George Leaman, the arranger from NBC. Why don't you and Alvino get married there? You can have someone you want perform the ceremony and your sisters can be your bridesmaids. We'll send out for a wedding cake and punch, and we'll do it up right!"

Dear, thoughtful Larry. I was beginning to see blue skies again.

That night in my lower berth on the night train to New York, I tried to sleep. I did feel better about my wedding day. Our bridal party would include my sisters and some of the boys in the band. Larry was going to sing my favorite song, "Springtime in Paris," and George was going to play the wedding march on his grand piano. We had called the president of the LDS mission in New York, and he consented to marry us. I would miss Mama and Daddy and Billy and Karleton and Maxine and Marilyn, but I would have Alyce, Donna, and Yvonne with me. It would be lovely and I could wear my new, cornflower-blue print silk dress and my matching blue straw hat.

But there was one problem we hadn't solved. What would we do about our religion? Until now we had just avoided talking about it, and thus, avoided fighting. Then a good feeling came over me. We would wait to see which religion would prevail, and if the Mormon faith were what I thought it to be, I would have no problems.

So with this positive thought, I dug my head in the pillow and listened to the clickety-clack of the rails and the mournful sound of the train whistle. "I must get some sleep," I thought, "for tomorrow is the big day — my wedding day."

The wedding ceremony in George Leaman's apartment was lovely. Alyce, my maid of honor, looked beautiful in the new outfit she was going to wear to Bermuda. Donna and Yvonne looked elegant, too. Alvino was spiffy in a beautiful new suit. Where did that come from? Had he secretly bought a new suit for his wedding? There were candles lit on the mantle and a gorgeous bouquet of long-stemmed yellow roses for the bride. Yellow roses are my favorite flower. (They were from Alvino and as time passes, he continues to be a very romantic, thoughtful husband. He has never missed an anniversary or special occasion. My sisters always hold him up as an example to their husbands.) But best of all there was a beautiful wedding cake, a little crumbled and smashed but made by my mother and sent special delivery. We all shed tears over that.

The president of the mission performed a beautiful Mormon wedding ceremony and I felt good and at peace with myself. After the wedding, the girls and the boys in the band rushed off to catch their boat to Bermuda and Alvino went to the garage to get our convertible.

I lay down in the bedroom and gave myself up to some pensive thoughts. A new chapter was beginning in my life. Would it be as happy and fine as my girlhood? It was up to me; I could make it that way. I closed my eyes and said a little prayer to my Heavenly Father and thanked him for all the happiness I had known. I fell asleep — but not for long — I was awakened by a kiss from my new husband.

"Come, Mrs. Rey, let's be off on our honeymoon," Alvino said, grabbing our bags. I picked up the yellow roses and Mama's beautiful wedding cake. We said our good-byes to George and Larry and thanked them for the use of their lovely apartment. We took the elevator down to the street floor and were soon in our Packard, headed down the East Coast to Virginia Beach. At last we were on our honeymoon!

Alvino's idea of a honeymoon was a trip to Kitty Hawk, North Carolina to see where the Wright Brothers first flew their little plane. I learned about that on the way to Virginia Beach. Being the type of girl I was, I went along with most of what Alvino suggested. For a wedding present, we both got third-degree burns from the hot sun and sands of Virginia Beach. Alvino got asthma and he hasn't had it since. I got what most young girls get once a month, I was lonesome for my sisters, lonesome for my folks and lonesome for the whole band. Consequently, when we returned to the Biltmore, I was still a sunburned, homesick virgin! Of course, that didn't last after we moved to our cozy, little apartment we had leased from a friend in New York City.

Sister Donna was going steady with Charlie Goodman, a young crooner in the band. He sang like Crosby. (Didn't everyone in those days?) Donna was the sweetheart of the band. She was sweet, friendly, sociable and Horace loved her — so did everyone else — Donna could do no wrong.

Yvonne was the firecracker of the group. She had more sex appeal than any young lady deserved to have. She was also temperamental and fiery and painfully truthful. Horace wasn't sure he liked that and sometimes wished he had Maxine back with the group. But Vonnie was the pin-up girl of the band and the college boys. Sometimes when the four of us would be singing, we'd look down at the young males and every eye would be fastened on Yvonne. The three of us could have stopped singing as far as the audience was concerned. She had a lot of film offers but never pursued a career on her own. I guess she needed her sisters around her to glorify her and make her shine.

Alyce was the real femme fatale of the group. She dated practically every good-looking big band trumpet player, the entire saxophone sections, the piano players and the arrangers. They all loved Alyce. They loved her beautiful eyes. They loved her soft, naturally curly, brown hair. They loved the way she moved and danced. They loved her sense of humor. If all the bands had been combined as a college, Alyce, without a doubt, would have been their homecoming queen.

The musicians loved Alyce's warm, beautiful, cello-like voice. But Alyce didn't try to make it on her own. I'm sure she could have done so because she had everything going for her. She could have been up there with the big singing stars —Ella Fitzgerald and the rest. But I guess it wasn't meant to be. She had an undying loyalty to her sisters and refused to leave us to strike out on her own.

As time went on, Alyce seemed to get continually more and more in the dog house with Horace. It was perplexing to us because we couldn't understand why. Horace had a way of picking at people if they became too popular. He did it with his accountant, his doctor, his wife, his girlfriends, and the members of the band. People were charmed by Alyce's voice and were prone to tell her so. The Stewart Warner sponsors told us that Alyce was responsible for our getting the Stewart Warner Radio Show. The wives of the sponsors loved the way Alyce sang "Stay as Sweet as You Are." Horace thought it was his duty to bring her down, or even attempt to break her spirit. If successful, he wouldn't have to give her a raise — not that he ever had.

The boys in the band and all of us were beginning to have more and more gripe sessions. We had been with him too long; we had paid our dues and we had cabin fever. Horace was becoming about as popular with the kids in the band as Captain Blye on the *Bounty*.

Heidt would hold meetings with the band and talk about how we could increase our popularity. Alvino would bring his Spanish guitar to the meeting and softly practice scales. He would never enter into the discussion. He had Heidt all figured out. He knew suggestions wouldn't be accepted; he knew Heidt only had these meetings to make people think they had a say in this "family band." And if they said the wrong thing, Heidt would immediately put them in the dog house. So Alvino kept quiet.

Bob Riedel, a tenor sax man in the band, really put himself in jeopardy. When asked if he had any suggestions about how we could improve the band, he said, "Mr. Heidt, I think everyone would speak more freely if you'd leave the room." Soon after that, honest Bob Riedel was fired.

We were beginning to think it about time for us to graduate from Mr. Heidt's college of life. The break culminated when a microphone accidently fell off its stand and hit a society dowager on the head. She was one of the hotel's most important patrons. Alyce was singing on the mike at the time. Horace was furious and fired Alyce on the spot.

That gave all of us an excuse to leave. Donna, Yvonne and I marched up to him and gave our notice. This was followed by Alvino doing the same. Sometime after that Frank DeVol, the talented young arranger, gave his notice and he was followed by several other members of the band. Horace couldn't believe what was happening. His whole band was falling apart! Poor Horace. With all his showmanship know-how and his salesmanship, he had underestimated the power of the female species!

But it was a good excuse to leave. We had plans to go back to the west coast and form our own band. Alvino would lead it, Frank DeVol would do the arranging and the King Sisters would sing. The band business was beginning to jump and we wanted to jump with it!

5

The Alvino Rey Band

"Honey, do you know that the band business is listed as one of the top money-making businesses in the country today?"

"Where did you read that?"

"Right here in the *Times.*"

"You know I don't have time to read the paper. You read it to me."

Alvino didn't miss a note on the scale as he talked. He was always practicing the guitar and I had to keep him posted on current events.

"Sunday, September 3, 1939. Chamberlain Takes Umbrella to Munich for Peace Conference . . ."

"No, I don't want to hear that. I've heard it ten times on the radio already. What more does it say about the band business?"

I read the article to Alvino. We were excited about it because we were going into that business ourselves. We had learned much from being with the Horace Heidt Band. We had watched him operate and saw how he turned his band into a big, money-making venture. We hoped we could do the same.

We were living in Los Angeles now. Alvino had just put his card in the L.A. musician's local and was waiting out the required six-month period. Radio Station KHJ offered him a job as a house band replacing Raymond Paige and his "California Melodies Hour." It would be a wonderful way to try out the exciting, new arrangements Frank DeVol was creating for the orchestra. We girls were practicing constantly. It was great not to be restricted by Horace anymore so we were trying far-out, four-part close harmonies and also doing some exciting original material.

One afternoon while we were diligently practicing in our little bungalow in the Hollywood hills, Spike Jones dropped in on us. He headed recordings for RCA Victor on the coast at the time. He was so impressed that he arranged an audition for us with Leonard Joy, the record producer for RCA in New York. That audition resulted in our first recording contract with Blue Bird and shortly after that, Al Pierce asked our quartet to join his gang at NBC. We did for awhile, but his show was much like Horace Heidt's and we were tired of that.

But we did get a thrill when Artie Shaw asked us to do the Old Gold Show with him for the summer. Artie's band was extremely popular. Artie, handsome and suave, had a romantic appeal with the ladies. They yelled and screamed and crowded and clutched at him whenever he appeared. All the clamoring didn't impress him for he was courting Betty Grable. I remember his purchasing a diamond for her and showing it to us to get our feminine approval.

Artie had a great, jumpy band with a lot of hits like "Begin the Beguine." His roster included Tony Pastor, Al Avola, Georgie Auld, Ray Conniff, and a young eighteen-year-old kid, named Buddie Rich. Buddy really pounded out the skins. We would have liked to stay with the "Old Gold Show" and Artie Shaw, but decided against it. We wanted to save ourselves for the great Alvino Rey Band which was soon to make its debut.

Alvino's Band made its first public appearance at the Civic

Auditorium in Pasadena. We were excited and overwhelmed when we saw how the place was packed with screaming, shouting teenagers. We knew we were on the right track. But we received some advice, something we already knew from big names in the business. If we really wanted to be successful, we must go east. That New York label was important again, only this time on our own band.

We didn't have the strength of the armies gathering across the Atlantic but we did have a lot of enthusiasm, hopes and dreams. We were determined to succeed. Our forces consisted of a handful of musicians, some instruments, and a suitcase full of songs and arrangements. And so in 1940, the Alvino Rey Band made its bid to capture the hearts of the New Yorkers. They were going to dance to our music and listen to our songs. We had an opening date at the famous Biltmore Hotel in the heart of Manhattan. Our strategy was faultless; there was no way we could fail. Our timing was just right — the big band era had arrived!

April 7, 1940 (from my diary)

> Well, here we go again! Our annual trek across the continent. Only this time, we don't know exactly when we will be returning, and so it was a tearful good-bye to Mama and Daddy and the rest of the family, with tear-filled eyes and red noses, and Alvino taking pictures of it all.
>
> Our caravan consists of three cars: a Lincoln Zephyr, loaded to the brim with baby bed, diapers, milk formulas, everything to make a little six-month old happy and contented. Dick "Icky" and Pam Morgan are taking their young baby with them to New York. Dick is going to play in Alvino's band. "Icky" got his nickname from Benny Goodman when they were playing together in the Benny Pollack Band in the late twenties. Members of the Pollack band had included Jack Teagarden and

Glenn Miller, as well as Benny Goodman. Benny had heard Dick call people that looked like "squares," "ickies" and made a funny little face. It broke Benny up and so he dubbed Dick "Icky," and it has stuck with him.

The second car in our caravan, a bright red Pontiac, is carrying my three younger sisters, two of which are quite light-hearted, but the third and youngest is sad indeed. She is leaving her darling Buddy behind and her poor little heart is broken. But I think the separation won't be for too long, as we certainly need Buddy Cole on the piano, even if he doesn't belong to the New York local.

Vonnie met Buddy Cole when she sang with Frankie Trumbauer for a short time after leaving Heidt. What a beautiful pianist he is, sort of a cross between Art Tatum and Teddy Wilson.

Alvino and I bring up the rear with our pale green Packard convertible which is loaded, not with babybeds or lovesick girls, but with guitars, guitars, and more guitars.

Music Corporation of America had booked us into the swank Biltmore Hotel in New York City, believing that we would do well because of our popularity with the Heidt Band, who had played there so long. What they didn't understand, was that our band was not the same as Heidt's. They found that out soon enough.

However, before our opening at the Biltmore, we had a break-in date in Hartford, Connecticut at the old Capitol Casino Gardens. It had been a strip joint, but had recently been turned into a showcase for big bands. We didn't mind joining the list of famous bands who had played there.

We were proud of the big band we had formed. We brought "Skeets" Herfurt with us. Skeets had played with Jimmie and Tommy Dorsey. A brilliant lead sax man, he had a sound like Marshall Royal who was with the Basie band, but in our opinion played better than Marshall. Skeets is still considered the finest lead sax in the band business and is currently playing with Lawrence Welk on his television show. Skeets is a musician who has devoted his entire life to his instrument.

Ickie Morgan joined us to play rhythm guitar and delighted the dancers with his funny antics. We had a fine brass section, headed by Frankie Strassek. With a great sax section headed by Skeets, a good rhythm section featuring Sandy Block on bass, and some brilliant, swinging original arrangements by Frank DeVol, and the *piece de resistance,* the four beautiful, young King Sisters who enchanted everyone with their personalities, freshness, and good musicianship, we were ready. And of course, fronting the band was Alvino Rey, virtuoso of every guitar known to mankind. The only way we could go was up with that entourage of talent.

But if we thought we were up, then we were soon to be put down, because every night at the Casino Gardens in Hartford the place was empty. The Gardens were run by two Italian gentlemen who were hospitable and friendly. They were also generous with their spaghetti but as our two-week engagement was devoid of patrons, we were literally paid off with it. This dismal news we received closing night. Oh well, there was always a rainbow ahead at the fabulous Biltmore!

The Biltmore received us with open arms — that is — until opening night. After hearing our loud, brassy arrangements, a little modern for the times, the management asked us politely if we could mute the band and play simple, sweet, society-type music. Naturally, we were disappointed, but we complied with their wishes. We'd had our fill of spaghetti and now needed "bread." We had a whole big band of salaries to meet and it was, indeed, a little scary.

We continued to play this hum-drum music for several weeks until one night a young fan came in to see us. He had heard some of our transcriptions made on the West Coast. There was one he particularly liked, "Tiger Rag," a novelty number that was exciting, fast, loud, and original. Would we play it?

Alvino looked down at Stu Woodruff's eager, smiling face. Alvino was tired of the elderly businessmen who wanted only a soft musical background while they talked business with their clients. Here was a young man who loved the music that we loved and who listened and danced to it with eager appreciation.

"Boys, take out the mutes and get out 'Tiger Rag.' " With that Alvino gave a big swoop on his electric guitar and the brass started roaring through Frank DeVol's exciting, original arrangement of "Tiger Rag." That piece did a lot for our band and has been copied by a lot of musicians, including Les Paul who made it a big hit on records. But it didn't do much for us that night at the Biltmore.

Mr. Mulligan, the manager of the hotel, was up in his suite. He wasn't as young as he used to be and was getting weary of the many late hours he had to keep. He had retired early, although it was only about 10:00 p.m., early for show people. He was lying in bed reading the *Wall Street Journal* when the sound came wafting in through the open windows on that summer night. What was that he was hearing? It sounded like a big jazz band from Harlem. It sounded like a bunch of trumpet players blowing their brains out. It sounded like that cheap jazz piece called "Tiger Rag." It couldn't be coming from the Biltmore Roof. It couldn't be that nice, quiet Alvino Rey who played soft Hawaiian steel guitar, nor could it be those lovely sisters who had harmonized so sweetly with Horace Heidt. What were they singing? "Here kitty, kitty, kitty; here kitty, kitty, kitty!"

Mr. Mulligan reached for his top coat, threw it over his silk pajamas and stormed up to the Biltmore Roof. Alvino and the boys had just finished the rip-roaring "Tiger Rag." Stu Woodruff and his young dancing companion were cheering and stomping their feet. The other young dancers were doing the same. The whole room was charged with an air of excitement.

Mr. Mulligan walked right up on to the bandstand, pajamas and all. His face was flushed and a pulsating vein stood out on his forehead.

"Mr. Rey, would you come over to the side of the room? I want to talk to you."

"Right now? I haven't finished the dance set," Alvino said meekly.

"Right now!" And Mr. Mulligan meant it.

The boys in the band started filing off the stand. I looked at Alvino. "Poor darling," I thought to myself. This was one of the joys of being a leader. (Alvino had to learn to take a lot of guff from owners of hotels and nightclubs and agents. Many times he had to keep it all to himself and not tell the boys in the band. It could break their spirits.)

It was late when Alvino got home to our apartment. I knew by the look on his face that it wasn't good news.

Mr. Mulligan had indeed fired the band on the spot. He didn't even want to give us a two-week notice. He thought he had hired a band like Horace Heidt's, a commercial society band that didn't get in the way of the New York businessmen and their background of soft, sweet music. The "Tiger Rag" arrangement was not what he had hired; the band had to go.

Alvino insisted that the band be given a two-week notice. It was a rule of the musicians' union so Mr. Mulligan had to concede.

Alvino gathered those who were partners in the Alvino Rey Band, Frank DeVol, Skeets Herfurt, and Icky Morgan, to talk it over at our apartment. They talked and talked into the early hours of the morning. No one had too many ideas about what to do with the band. It was discouraging. Alvino didn't want to tell the girls. They might want to go home, back to California and the good life, especially Vonnie and Buddy — they were planning to get married the next week.

"Oh, honey, let's not tell them. Let's not spoil the wedding. We'll tell them when they get back from their honeymoon," I said.

He agreed and the wedding went on unspoiled by the bad news.

Vonnie had bought a beautiful pale, pink sheer gown with layers of ruffles from Loehman's in Yonkers. It was a house where you could get dresses for practically wholesale prices. Yvonne was always good at finding bargains. She looked beautiful in it, like something out of *Gone With the Wind.*

The girls had leased a spacious home in Yonkers for we had expected we would be playing the Biltmore for the entire summer. The folks had come back with Billy and Marilyn and planned to spend some time with their daughters. Mama was unhappy at seeing her little Vonnie getting married at the age of 18.

"Vonnie, why don't you and Buddy wait a few years. You're so very young. You don't know what life is all about," Mama had said.

"Oh, but Buddy and I want to be as happy as Luise and Alvino are. Why should we wait?" Vonnie was an impetuous, little pixie and certainly lacked my patience.

It rained on Vonnie and Buddy's wedding day. It rained so hard that the wedding party had to come into the house for the ceremony. The rain completely ruined Daddy's elaborate flower arbor he had created for the garden wedding. It rained on Vonnie's day and throughout her married life with Buddy. Their marriage ended in stormy divorce. It lasted long enough, however, for them to produce two lovely, talented daughters and some wonderful, happy memories of Buddy Cole.

He was a sensitive artist, and we loved going to the studio in his backyard where he had installed a huge theatre pipe organ. When he played it, the walls of the little studio vibrated with such power and glorious sound, we felt as if we were on our way to heaven.

Buddy was also a comic but Vonnie found it wasn't fun to be married to him. She once said, "Buddy, why don't we do things together like Luise and Alvino? We don't seem to enjoy the same things."

One morning when Buddy was still sleeping, Vonnie decided to take out the trash and was being a little noisy about it. Buddy awoke and rushed out to help her.

"You see Vonnie, we do too do things together," he said with a roguish smile.

That was Buddy for you, but Buddy was not for Vonnie.

Even on the wedding night, the show had to go on, so Marilyn, ten years old, took Vonnie's place and made her debut with the King Sisters. She was a big smash. We gave Vonnie and Buddy two nights off in the Poconos for a honeymoon. When the lovers returned, they found that we had lost the job at the Biltmore due to the "Tiger Rag" episode. We cancelled the lease on the Yonkers house, sent the folks home, and gloom set in.

6

New Jersey

It was a gloomy period but we weren't going to let it make us give up. I was worried about the girls, though. Alyce became depressed easily, and she could influence Donna and Yvonne. What could we do to make them want to stick around New York until we got another job? How could we hold this twelve-piece band together? I had an idea.

"Alvino, you know how the girls like parties and picnics and people? We could have a get-together every day until we get a job."

"Who's got the money for that?" Alvino asked. Unlike most bands of the day, we had no angel to look to for sustenance. Our band was a co-operative organization. Alvino, Frank DeVol, Skeets Herfurt, Icky Morgan and the King Sisters all owned a piece of it. None of us had put any money into it, just our talents, and now we were finding out that talent couldn't buy groceries or pay the rent. We didn't want to borrow money because we had been taught by Daddy and Mama never to borrow.

"It doesn't have to cost that much," I said. "We really don't have room for all of them in our tiny apartment. We'll do it in the park. The girls will help. They love to cook. If we pool our resources, it will work. Instead of sitting around with long faces, we can have fun."

Alvino agreed and we did have fun. We cooked chili beans and hot dogs, fried potatoes and hamburgers, spaghetti and stew. The smell of that food in the open air was delightful. We played games, silly games like charades and run, sheepy, run. We sang and harmonized and Alvino accompanied us on his guitar. We laughed until we were sick. Paul Weston and Axel Stordahl and Jack Egan from Tommy Dorsey's band joined us, and once we got Tommy to be in a homemade movie we concocted.

We had about three days of this frivolity, and then we got the phone call we were expecting. Daily, Alvino had been in touch with our friend Russ Lyons at MCA trying to get work for the band. It wasn't easy after the big flop at the Biltmore. MCA was a little wary of us, but Russ believed in us and we knew he would come up with something if only our lean bank account would hold out long enough.

Russ called Alvino on the phone. "Alvino, we've got an engagement for the band! It's at the Syracuse Hotel in Syracuse, New York. The band they had booked has cancelled. You can start this Friday."

"Well, I don't know whether we should play in a hotel. I'm a little afraid of it. Maybe a ballroom or roadside club would be better." Alvino didn't want a repeat of the Biltmore failure.

"They'll love you. It's a college town, you know. They've been playing your transcriptions. In fact, the kids have been screaming for you." Russ talked in a cheerful, managerial voice, trying to reassure us.

Russ was right. We took the job and we were a big success. The kids jammed the hotel and crowded the bandstand. They requested their favorites and loved whatever we did. Life was good again. We were "in" and we knew it.

Our next engagement was the Rustic Cabin in Englewood

Cliffs, New Jersey. The girls didn't want to take the engagement; they wanted to go home to California, even after the success at Syracuse. But Alvino and I talked them in to staying in the East. We had a hunch it would be good for our career and we were right. A skinny boy singer by the name of Frank Sinatra had just left the Rustic Cabin to join the new, swinging Harry James Band. We felt this was a good opportunity.

We didn't get paid much at the Rustic Cabin. The boys in the band each got thirty-five dollars a week while the King Sisters and Alvino only took thirty. We played it mainly for experience, fun and the air time it provided. We got all three in abundance. As I look back at it now, it was a wonderful, happy time of our lives, and was the real start of our career in the big band business.

A large, three-story colonial house sat back off a circular driveway which was lined with beautiful blue spruce trees. The real estate agent said it had been for rent for some time, but it was too large for most people. There was no furniture in it but its location was just right for us — off Highway 9W, a few miles from the Rustic Cabin. Alvino and I got the bright idea that we could get enough beds, chairs and tables from Bekin's Storage nearby to furnish the house in sort of a makeshift way. There were really no hotels in Englewood Cliffs, and this home was large enough to house our whole band. We had to be close to where we worked because WOR Mutual Network had promised us a lot of air time if we could be on call as a stand-by if the ball games were rained out. It was much too far to commute from New York daily and besides, the George Washington Bridge toll would cost us more than we would make.

We put a deposit on the house and the realtor gave us the key. We thought we were all set — until the owner of the house showed up. Four pairs of blue eyes looked into the brown eyes of a plump, Italian gentleman.

"Ver' sorry. You nice young ladies. But I don' wanna rent 'cha my house!"

"But the house has been for rent for years and the real estate man has taken our money and given us the keys," we looked up at him imploringly.

"I know, I know, but all 'dos boys in the band livin' here. I got valuable stuff stored in basement and I know how young musicians are. Dey'd probably wreck 'da joint!"

"Oh! But we're different. Really we are. We're just one big family."

"Ha! And I suppose you all have the same Mama and Papa?"

"Yes and no. We girls do and we feel it's our responsibility for the boys in our band to lead a good, healthy, normal home life when they are working for us. Some of them have never had a home. That's why we loved your place. We thought we could make it a real home for our boys."

Alyce's big, blue eyes started spilling over with tears. Vonnie, Donna and I soon followed suit.

With that, the Italian gentleman took out a big, white handkerchief and blew his nose. (I had always heard that Italians were a sentimental lot. There were a couple of them in our band.)

"All right, all right. We like our families, too. Tell ya' what. You stay here one month. If 'dos boys don' behave themselves, out ya' go!"

We stayed there for almost a year, and we never learned what was in the basement. But our landlord had a heart of gold. He became a good friend for years to come. He told us he was never sorry he rented us the house.

We loved playing the Rustic Cabin. It was just an overgrown hot dog stand with red-checkered tablecloths and moose heads hanging on the wall but the kids came there in droves, and they loved the band. We were left completely alone by the management, so different from our engagement at the Biltmore. We played just the way we wanted to. We played for the kids, and we were always on the air, even when there were blizzards and bad weather.

One particular Sunday afternoon the WOR radio technician

was unable to make his way through the storm for our broadcast but that didn't keep us from going on the air. Alvino, who had quite a flair for electronics and with the help of Buddy Cole, figured out how to do it. When the engineer finally showed up, we were just going off the air. The engineer and the radio station personnel were quite amazed. But that's how it was—we never missed a broadcast!

Laughter, fun, and music rang through the "Chateau" (as we called it) that winter. Our young friends who frequented the Rustic Cabin often stopped by after work for scrambled eggs or spaghetti. I don't know how we managed feeding our own "family" plus all our guests, because we only charged the boys $10 a week for room and board. But that was in the days when bread cost five cents and help could be had for a song. We hired two black maids, one to cook and one to clean. We paid them each $10.00 per week.

We also had our share of professional friends enter our lives during the Chateau period. Kenny Gardner, who later married one of the Lombardo girls and is still singing with the Lombardo Band, was dating Donna. Myrt of the famed "Myrt and Marge" radio show was our neighbor. Her Sunday afternoon open house was a regular "who's who" for Broadway and radio celebrities. Ozzie and Harriet would stop by for hot chocolate and discuss the problems of the big band business. I think Ozzie got a lot of ideas for his "Adventures with Ozzie and Harriet" series right there in his little neighborhood home in Tenafly, New Jersey. We also met two young men at the Cabin who were later to become the husbands of my sisters. Jim Conkling, who married Donna, was to become president of Capitol Records, Warner Brothers and Columbia, and later headed the "Voice of America" program. When we first met him, he was a cute, blonde school boy from Maplewood, New Jersey. Alyce later married Syd de Azevedo, who became a big shipping prexie, but was just a handsome school kid from Rutherford, New Jersey. He had just dropped in at the Rustic Cabin for a drink. And my sisters hadn't really wanted to take the Rustic Cabin engagement. How different their lives would have been if we hadn't insisted!

Spring came to Englewood Cliffs and what a beautiful spring it was. That was our first encounter with the eastern countryside, having been confined to the big cities and hotels during most of our sojourn in the band days. Fragrant lilac bushes lined the road, all the trees were in bloom, and we watched and sang about apple blossom time.

But the world was being torn apart with that big, ugly war in Europe. Roosevelt was still being hated by the Republicans and loved by the Democrats. One of the best-loved ballads we sang was called "My Sister and I," which was about two little Jewish refugees who had sailed to the United States after their mother and father had both been brutally killed in the concentration camps in Germany. I don't think we really understood the terrible message in that song as we sang it nightly from the bandstand.

We also made a big hit of "A-One in the Army and He's A-One in My Heart," written by Red Evans. Red wrote many of the popular songs of the day including, "Dance, Ballerina, Dance." There was beginning to be a sprinkling of military uniforms in our audience but the war really hadn't touched us yet. We were living in a beautiful bubble of music, dancing, and song, and hadn't begun to feel the ugliness of the world around us.

7

The Big Time

The spring of 1941, in spite of all the rumblings of war, was romantic and exciting to us.

The romantic part was the wedding of Alyce and Syd de Azevedo which we were helping to plan. The wedding was going to be held at the beautiful home of Mayor Coffin of Englewood, New Jersey. Mama and Daddy were driving all the way east and bringing the rest of the family. We hadn't seen them for over a year.

It was wonderful seeing the folks again. Maxine and Karleton didn't come back as they were busy with their jobs and new spouses, but Mama and Daddy had brought Billy and Marilyn. How baby Marilyn had grown. She was longlegged and looked like a young colt. We agreed she was going to be the tallest one in the family, and she was beautiful. To think that Mama hadn't been too happy about that change-of-life baby. And Marilyn could sing!

She imitated Ella Mae Morse to perfection and what a flair for comedy. Mama and Daddy weren't going to be able to keep her home too long; she had one foot on the stage already.

Little brother Billy wasn't so little any more, either. He had developed into a teenager and loved big bands. Although he was talented at music, and wrote cute songs, some of which we recorded later, his real talent was as an artist and cartoonist. He loved to draw and sat by the hour creating funny little characters and ideas.

We often received picturesque letters from him with sketches of the band and with Alvino and the King Sisters appearing at number one spots in the nation: "Alvino Rey and the King Sisters Wow Them at the Coconut Grove," "King Sisters and Alvino Rey Sensational at the Paramount Theatre," "Alvino Rey and the King Sisters Have Them Jumping at the Paladium," "King Sisters and Alvino Rey Appear in Socko Picture for RKO." He had dreams and a lot of enthusiasm and proved to be a better prophet than any of us knew. Alvino offered him a job as a band boy and he enjoyed doing that for a couple of summers when he was vacationing from school.

Alyce was excited to introduce Mama and Daddy to Syd.

"Mom and Dad, this is Syd," she said proudly. "I did what you told me to do, Daddy. I waited and I got the very best!"

Syd was the very best. He was tall and handsome and very clean-cut looking. Although his father was Brazilian, Syd took after his New England mother's side of the family. He was fair of skin with dark brown curly hair, an intellect, a graduate of Hamilton College. He loved music, was a magnificent dancer, and he idolized Alyce. Being the son of a shipping magnate, it was amazing how unspoiled he was. He was humble and friendly to everyone. People loved him—from the gas attendant at the local service station, to the bus boys at his favorite restaurant. Even the prexies at his father's plush Manhattan office thought him a fine young man.

It was hard for Mama and Daddy to see most of their girls marry outside their cherished religion. Goodness knows Daddy had tried his best to convert the young men we had fallen in love with. However, those long, complicated epistles of religious philosophy Daddy had written to them hadn't worked. But our parents weren't going to give up and kept hoping for the day a miracle would happen. In the meantime, they loved and supported their new sons-in-law and believed them to be fine young men.

While Alyce and Syd were away for a short honeymoon, baby sister Marilyn was going to sing with us. Syd had enlisted in the army in order to get his "year" over with and had put in for a furlough.

It was a beautiful June morning and Mayor Coffin's garden was alive with daffodils, tulips, and lilacs. Lilacs were Alyce's favorite flower. I was matron of honor and wore a flowing, white sheer frock with the lilac skirt handpainted by Yvonne and accented by a lilac-colored picture hat. I had neglected myself for my own wedding, but I compensated for it at this one.

It was unusually hot for that season of the year. I noticed Alyce's face was flushed and beads of perspiration were standing out on Syd's forehead. He must have been miserable in that cut-away coat and grey striped trousers, but they were formally correct so I knew Alyce was happy.

A group of musicians from the band, including Skeets Herfurt, was playing chamber music at the beginning of the ceremony. Suddenly a playful breeze whipped the music from his music stand and Skeets started following it down the path just as the bridal party was entering. Skeets was a foggy, lovable musician whose only concern was following the music and he didn't miss a note. It was a comical sight and soon everyone was laughing uproariously.

The ceremony continued with an air of merriment that somewhat destroyed the formal atmosphere so loved by Alyce. But it took everybody's mind off the hot weather and we were all delighted to see Alyce married to her wonderful Syd.

Our first big crack at the "big time" started with a telephone call from our good friend Jack Egan, who had just begun acting as our manager. Jack was a jovial sort of person who was a close buddy of Tommy and Jimmy Dorsey, Ozzie and

Harriet, and countless other band leaders, publishers, and musicians. He always knew everything that was going on in the band business.

"Girls — Dinah Shore has a severe case of laryngitis and can't finish her engagement at the Paramount Theatre. I suggested to Bob Wietman that they use you and they are willing to try it. Could you be at the theatre around eleven o'clock, go over your tunes with Charlie Barnet between shows, and do the two o'clock show?"

"But, Jack, it takes more than half an hour to get to New York! What'll we wear? What'll we sing?" My three sisters were huddled around the phone trying to hear what Jack was saying to me. We were all talking at once!

"Well, hang up and that will give you more time to decide. I'll meet you at the stage entrance on 44th."

Within the allotted time we were on the Paramount Stage, costumed, made-up, singing, and swinging our hearts out. "In the Mood," "Jersey Bounce," "I'll Get By," and "I Understand" were all part of our repertoire. Up until the Paramount appearance, we didn't have the slightest idea what all the air time at the Rustic Cabin had done for us. But our fans knew; they yelled and screamed and shouted and requested their favorite numbers. We couldn't get off the stage. We couldn't believe how well they knew and liked us! Why, we were famous and loved and we didn't even know it!

Charlie Barnet and his unknown-at-that-time girl singer, Lena Horne, came back to our dressing room to congratulate us. Charlie brought a big cake (it was his birthday) and a photographer from *Down Beat,* a music magazine, appeared and took pictures of us sharing the cake. Bob Wietman, the manager of Paramount, announced he wanted to sign us for a return engagement, but next time with Alvino Rey and the band. We rushed to the pay phone backstage to call Daddy and Mama and tell them the good news!

We grabbed the handful of quarters we kept for making phone calls and slipped them one by one into the quarter slot of the pay phone. The operator came on, and I gave the Oakland number of our folks. It rang once, it rang twice, and then Mama's dear voice came through the receiver.

"Hello."

"Is this you, Mama?"

"Yes, is this Luise? Is something wrong? Why are you calling us long distance? Is Alyce sick? Is anything wrong with Yvonne?"

Mama, the worrier, always suspected the worst.

"No, nothing is wrong with any of us. We're backstage at the Paramount Theatre. We just finished a show."

"Backstage at the Paramount? You mean that big theatre on Times Square? What are you doing there?"

"We just got off the stage. We subbed for Dinah Shore who was ill. The kids in the audience loved us so much, they wouldn't let us leave the stage. They knew every song we sang. It was so exciting. Mama, we've finally made the big time!"

"Just a minute. I want to get your father. You must tell him all about it."

Now Daddy was on the line, and I let Alyce tell the story this time. She was a good storyteller and was prone to exaggerate and be more colorful than I. Then Donna and Yvonne got their two cents in and our three minutes were up—but not before Daddy said "Don't forget to tell them whose daughters you are!"

Soon after that we got our first royalty check from RCA Victor. As we tore the check out of the envelope and quickly glanced at it, we thought it was for four dollars. Then we thought it must be for forty dollars. As we looked at the zeroes more carefully, we realized the check was for four thousand dollars. We couldn't believe it! How should we spend all that money? After much talking and discussion, we finally agreed on a plan. We were going to buy each of us a mink coat—four beautiful, dark, real mink coats. From the day we began working, we had sent money home and actually supported the rest of the family. We had bought them a lovely Stewart Warner radio so they could hear us from Chicago. We had bought them a new General Electric refrigerator. We had bought Mama a nice grey squirrel stole and baby Marilyn a white bunny coat, but this time, the money was manna from heaven and we were going to give ourselves a much needed treat. Besides, if we wanted to be big stars, we needed to look the part. We wanted to look classy.

And so it was the big time from then on for us and the band. It was the Astor Roof and the Meadowbrook. It was the Paladium and the Sherman Hotel and the Totem Pole. It was one-nighters, thousands of them, Boston, Scranton, Hershey Park, Columbus, Omaha, Salt Lake, Philadelphia, Los Angeles—wherever the kids wanted to dance and swing, we went.

A major part of the time, a Greyhound bus was our home. When it wasn't parked behind a ballroom, it could be found parked at the gourmet restaurant Alvino had handpicked for us or perhaps heading up a mountain road en route to a picnic, a spot we girls would have chosen. We sisters were anxious to introduce our pale-faced city boys to the wonders and glories of nature, the way our father had shown us when we were kids.

Big bands now were considered big business and it was a tough job to be the leader. Alvino soon learned he had to keep a respectable distance from the musicians. Some leaders had the reputation of being downright nasty to their men. Benny Goodman was well known for his "evil eye" and the musicians would quake in their boots if they were the recipient of "the look." Tommy Dorsey had a bad disposition and fought with his brother, Jimmy, as well as with the men in his band. And Glenn Miller was no doll. He was stern and unrelenting.

The sweethearts among the band leaders were Woody Herman, Stan Kenton and Alvino Rey. The musicians loved to play in Alvino's band. Through the portals of his orchestra passed many young men who later made their marks in the music business. Billy May, Frank DeVol, Ray Conniff, Johnny Mandel, Niel Hefti, Jimmy Joyce, Andy Russel, Mel Lewis are just a few of the arrangers, musicians, and singers who enjoyed working with him and Alvino is proud to be remembered affectionately by them.

A music critic of the band days recently sent us this article:

February 15, 1983

REY MUSICIANS FORM FRIENDSHIPS

by Glen Martin

If there ever was a close family of musicians and singers, it was found in the cadre of Alvino Rey and his orchestra. This could be attributed to their lasting friendships and respect for each other that came about during the tenure of the Rey band.

In 1939, Alvino asked Frank DeVol to write the book for his band. Being a top flight arranger, DeVol in no time gave the band a most captivating sound that featured Rey on his famous electronic guitar.

The King Sisters were indeed brilliant in their vocal work. They caught the imagination of the public as did the Andrews Sisters. The bank had some fine musicians, singers, and arrangers that were to be heard from in later years. These people are as close as a family of friends could be to this day."

And so were the big band days in full swing, with the headaches, the heartaches, the gags and the laughs. Musicians have always been known for their great capacities for enjoyment and their keen senses of humor.

Our lifelong, good friend Frank DeVol is a marvelous comedian. He could have been another Bob Newhart had he concentrated on comedy instead of music. As it is, he had appeared on a number of TV series as a comic. Our friend Billy May is well known for his clever, caustic remarks. Buddy Cole was as glib and funny as a man could be. Bill Richmond, who played drums for Alvino, became a writer for Carol Burnett and moved up to be a TV producer in Hollywood. Our association with these young men, our band buddies, certainly made life on the road more tolerable. Although there were times when the going was rough, I will say one thing — there was never a dull moment!

8

The Bus

After playing a dance spot for almost six months, the band would begin itching to get on the road. The musicians became restless after being cooped up that long. They would get bored playing for the same people and they looked forward to "hitting the road." The leader was always anxious to start the one-nighters because it was here he would make his money and recoup some of what he lost while playing a little spot that couldn't possibly pay what the band was worth. But these spots were important to play because a band would get air time — which was pure gold. The more air time a band had, the more popular it became. But it was with the one-nighters that the leader really got a chance to meet his big public — his fans — and to feel the excitement of show business.

The big ballrooms were fun to play. Here the kids really let go and danced. And how they would dance! Young people seemed to feel the pulse of the big band and they jitterbugged. The band felt the pulse of the jitterbugging and caught the fever. By midnight, the ballrooms were "roaring" and so was the band.

To tour between these one-nighters, most bands found it best to use a Greyhound bus. Of course some of those jumps were terrible. There was a story going around among the boys in the band that MCA, the biggest of the band booking offices, would sit in their plush decorated offices and throw darts at a map of the United States and wherever the darts landed, that was where they would send the band. And many times it seemed to be the way it was.

It was a gypsy life and the bus was our home. Many times after playing a dance job, we would have to drive all night to make the next engagement. We would enter the bus after playing a one-night stand and start an arduous trip to the town of our next engagement. Everyone would be keyed up after playing all night. If the band had jived and played well, there would be a lot of enthusiasm in the air; but if they hadn't, there would be bickering and arguing. The sax would blame the brass, the brass would blame the rhythm, the piano player would blame the bass, and the bass would blame the drummer, and the leader would blame anyone he felt like blaming. If the boys were late getting back on the stand, he would blame the road manager who was generally one of the musicians. The road manager always took a lot of guff from the leader. He also took a lot of guff from his fellow musicians. It was a hard life for him and he generally ended up neglecting his instrument and sometimes, if he got too enamored with his managing, he gave up his music and went into the managing business. After all, there was more money in managing than playing in a band.

The musicians would be hot and perspiring after playing all night. They would hang up their uniforms in the back of the bus and get into their comfortable traveling clothes. They would open a can of beer and light a cigarette and try to relax. After all, this was the end of their day—but it really wasn't—they had a long night of travel ahead of them. The back of the bus always smelled gamey, like a locker room.

That's why we girls sat up front with the leader and boy singer. We very seldom removed our makeup. We were too vain. But by the time we arrived at our destination, our eye makeup would be smudged, our lipstick smeared, our hair a mess. Our vanity really didn't pay off.

When we would begin the tour of one-nighters, everyone would be in a good mood. The band was always glad to be on the road again. They welcomed a change of scenery. A few of them were glad to get away from their wives so they could swing again. It was exhilarating to be out on the road, to see new places and new people. Musicians tend to be restless and need a certain amount of freedom.

But after about three weeks of being on the road, everyone would start to get bus fever, especially when the jumps started getting too long and the guys got tired. It was funny, though, the more tired the band got on the road, the better they played. They seemed to swing better when they were beat.

Sometimes there were mistakes when the booking office sent the band to the wrong town. Once after a long all-night ride through a blinding snow storm, we arrived at the little town of North Hills, Pennsylvania. It was seven in the morning and the sun came glaring in through the dirty windshield. We were awakened by the sound of the bus driver and the road manager arguing. The bus driver and the manager were pouring over a map.

"Yeah, this is North Hills all right. It's a suburb of Philadelphia. That black dot right next to the big red circle," says the manager.

"But man, this town doesn't have a ballroom. I know. I've been here before. I drove Les Brown here last month. They have a college, but not a ballroom." The driver was sure of himself.

"I'll run into this service station and ask them where the Rainbow Ballroom is." The manager didn't believe the driver.

By this time, the whole band was awake. We were watching the manager and the service station attendant. The attendant was shaking his head and pointing south. The manager walked back to the bus looking dejected and tired. He spoke to the bus driver.

"You're right. There is no Rainbow Ballroom here. It's in

North Hills all right, but Pennsylvania has two North Hills. The Rainbow Ballroom is in North Hills in southern Pennsylvania about 300 miles from here."

The griping began. Everyone was edgy and cranky.

"You mean we've gone 300 miles out of our way? I don't believe it."

"That damn MCA. Why don't they put the correct information on the contract?"

"That damn driver. Why doesn't he find out where he's going before he starts on a long haul like this?"

"That damn manager, he doesn't even play good bass any more. It's his fault for not checking and double checking with MCA."

"I've just got to have my sleep. If I don't get eight hours, I'll lose my voice and then none of us can sing. I've got the lead."

"Can't we check into a hotel for a few hours? I'm beat."

"I've got to get a cup of coffee. I'm freezing to death back here. Why can't we get heat in the back of the bus?"

"I'm roasting to death. It's so hot up here in the front. Willie, can't you turn off the heat?"

"This is the last road tour I'm going to do with this band. I got a call from Freddie Martin out on the coast. He stays at the Grove for six months at a time. There you can have an apartment and spend your days sitting in the sunshine."

And the griping went on and on and the poor bus driver went on and on, but this time in the right direction.

The bus drivers were a show by themselves. Most of them were pretty good guys who did their jobs well. But some of them were real characters. We had one who had a habit of disappearing just as we were ready to leave. One time, after much searching, we found him with the classy dame he had dated for the evening and was loathe to leave her. He wanted to take her in the bus with him but that was against the rules of the road so his idea was nixed. A couple of times we found the driver dead drunk in his hotel room. He was put in a shower and sobered up before we continued our trip. Of course, we couldn't put up with that and he found himself without a job as soon as he could be replaced. But most of the drivers were good guys who did their job well — and it was hard work. They all seemed to like to talk and they kept everyone around them—as well as themselves—awake by telling tall tales of their experiences driving the big bands around the country.

One driver told us funny stories about what went on in some of the buses — terrible stories about how the girl singers and boys in the band behaved — especially some of the big jazz bands. Through it all, the stalwart bus driver kept driving on through sleet and snow, rain and fog, trying to make his destination.

Sometimes during the night, everyone but the driver would get settled down and there would be a few hours of sleep before the sun came glowing through the windshield. We would arrive at the hotel to check in, have a bath, a little rest, eat, then play the gig in the strange little town and move on again. Four weeks of this life was about as much as anyone could stand. A lot of the bands kept going for months, and then the musicians would start griping more and more and the leader would know it was time to settle down and play a regular spot before he lost his whole band.

It was a gypsy life, but we loved it. Thanks to our father, we had been gypsies when we were kids so we may have been better prepared than some.

Childhood Scene

By 1924 most American families owned an automobile and on Sundays, nearly all of those families were out for a drive. At home, most people enjoyed themselves by listening to the radio. In 1924 the National Broadcast Company organized the first network and before long twelve million American families were listening in. Some people even had vacuum cleaners, washing machines, and electric refrigerators. We didn't have those luxuries but we did have a beautiful grand piano!

Daddy had been a school teacher in Utah right after World War I. He had come to Ephraim to find a house to rent as he would be teaching music at the Snow Normal College that fall. He found a lovely, old, red brick house and sent for us to join him.

Daddy greeted us at the front door. We looked around our new home, especially Mama. The house was entirely devoid of furniture. Only a full-size grand piano sat proudly in the living room. Our furniture was to have been shipped from our last home in Colorado and should have been waiting for us.

"King, there's no furniture, no beds, no tables, no anything — only this piano! What happened to everything you were to have shipped?" Mama's eyes were beginning to fill with tears. She was very emotional and prone to cry easily, a trait we seemed to inherit.

"Pearl, man cannot live by bread alone. After I bought the piano in Salt Lake, I just didn't have enough money to have the furniture shipped. But it will be all right, honey. I have an idea. Let's go camping in the beautiful Utah mountains for the summer and by fall my salary will start, and we'll be able to send for the furniture."

Of course, we children loved the idea, all five of us. We yelled and screamed with delight. We loved the out-of-doors, and we thought a summer of camping would be divine. Mama wasn't so sure, but what else could she do?

Daddy went over to the piano and started playing and singing the new hit song "Ain't We Got Fun." We all chimed in when Daddy started in with his big bass voice, and the house seemed warm and fun even without furniture. Mama went into the kitchen and found a large black stove there. If she could get King to stop singing to build a fire, she could heat the cold chocolate we'd brought with us on the train. There were some sandwiches left in the picnic hamper that would do for supper. Thank heavens she had brought Grandma's quilts with us. We could bed down in front of the fire and be rather cozy. And we did just that. It was good to be together with Daddy again.

In the morning Daddy and Mama went uptown and got the supplies for the camping trip. The storekeeper assured them that there would be folks going back and forth to the mountains that summer so Daddy could get a ride into town to replenish our supplies.

We spent the summer in the Emery Mountains just above Ephraim, and it was a wonderful summer. We brought with us the jersey cow that came with the red brick house and thus were the envy of all the other campers. Daddy was good at making us comfortable out in the open. He knew how to make soft beds out of pine needles, and he fashioned a table and benches of rough pine, and they served rather nicely for an outdoor family room. Our ceiling was a crystalline clump of stars. The fragrance of the pine trees and campfire permeated our mountain home. Mama did most of the cooking but Daddy always made French toast for breakfast. "You can eat it with your hands and save a lot of dishes," he said. In the afternoon we would take long nature walks, exploring the countryside. He would explain every wildflower and tree along the way. The evenings were the best time of all because that's when we'd sit around the campfire and sing and tell stories. Daddy was a marvelous storyteller and kept us entertained with his boyhood memories. The story we liked best was the one about how he and Mama had met. He told it as if he were reading a novel, with romance and detail. How we loved it!

Daddy had just graduated from the BYU Academy in Provo, Utah. He was president of the Class of 1907. His first job was a school teaching assignment in the little town of Sanford, Colorado. To get there, he had to take an uncomfortable and jerky narrow gauge railroad and sleep sitting up in a chair car for two nights. He was rudely awakened by the conductor shouting over the sound of the rails, "Wake up, young man, this is LaJara, Colorado, the end of the line. You're going to have to get off here."

Daddy aroused himself from his dream. It wasn't a fine concert hall in New York City. And the sound of applause he had heard in his dream was nothing but the clattering of train wheels hitting the rails.

Daddy rubbed his smarting eyes. They were not accustomed to the smoky, cigar-smelling chair car. He ran his fingers through his unkempt hair. Three days and two nights in a chair car that reeked of baby's urine, tobacco smoke, and stale apples was more than his immaculate nature could endure. His bones were aching; he felt like a man of seventy. He longed for a nice hot bath. His new blue serge suit was a crumpled mess. Well, it could be pressed as good as new, he supposed, if he could find someone to do it in this God-forsaken wilderness. He looked for his briefcase, the shiny new case that the class of

"07" had presented to him as their class president. He hoped nobody had latched onto it while he was sleeping. "Ah, there it is," he patted it reassuringly. The car was practically deserted with the exception of one struggling, young mother, yanking at two bawling infants. The conductor finally came to her rescue.

Daddy pulled at his collar trying to make it look more respectable, and unraveling his lanky legs, stood up and reached for his bowler and squared it on his head. Clutching his bulging brief case, he strolled out of the dingy chair car.

Daddy stood on the desolate train platform of LaJara, Colorado, the fine prairie sand and wind cutting at his body. He clutched his briefcase, not wanting to lose any of its precious contents.

"Damn this Colorado climate! No wonder the United States gave it to the Mexicans and Indians." The wind, cold and piercing, pushed and unbalanced him.

Two Colorado sheep men in dirty overalls and mackinaws huddled in the doorway of the crude train station and rolled their cigarettes. Daddy thought he saw a smurky look on their faces. They were probably making fun of the city dude in his new blue suit and black bowler. So these were the kinds of people he had to teach! There wasn't even a buggy there to meet him. He'd just have to walk to Sanford. It was only eight miles. His legs needed stretching after that three-day train trip anyway. It appeared he was going to have to show these country hicks a few things. He picked up his briefcase and started the trek to Sanford, Colorado — population five hundred.

Daddy walked into the Sanford general store. It was a dismal and gloomy contrast to the vivid Colorado sunshine he had just left. It was a typical country store, overstuffed and overflowing with bags of flour, sugar, calico goods, shoes, straw hats and penny candy.

A group of overalled farmers crowding around a potbellied stove, looked at him suspiciously as he entered. Daddy scanned the establishment for the storekeeper. He finally discovered a slight figure of a man with a receding chin, pointed nose, and thinning, greyish hair. The man was huddled over a desk.

Daddy walked up to him and cleared his throat, hoping to get his attention. The man didn't look up but kept adding a long line of figures on a store ledger. Daddy waited patiently and then put on his best actorish voice.

"Sir, I was wondering if you could tell me where I might find lodging of some kind."

The storekeeper gave him a quick once-over. He looked dubiously at Daddy's new high-buttoned shoes, his crumpled suit, and the new bowler.

'I'm sorry, if you're looking for a hotel, we don't have one here. Never had any use fer one, you see we're just plain, hardworking, God-fearing folks. The closest hotel is in Alamosa eight miles away. That's where the travelin' men stay."

Daddy could tell that the storekeeper didn't warm up to newcomers and felt his animosity.

"Oh, but you see I'm not a traveling man! I'm the new music teacher your school board has hired. I have to live here in Sanford. I've got to have room and board and a piano." Daddy was thinking that the piano was more important than room and board. His fingers already felt stiff from several days without practicing.

"The only piano we got is over at the school house. We work too hard to sit around playing the piano at night. We're tired and we go to bed when the sun sets, like the good Lord intended. No use burning expensive oil until midnight."

Daddy later found out that the storekeeper, besides being practical, was just plain stingy. His heart sagged! So this was what it would be. This was why he had scrimped and saved so that he could study at the Academy in Provo. And now, his lofty dream of setting the world on fire with glorious music he had composed, was trailing in the dust. Four long years of denying himself pleasures that other students seemed to enjoy were for nothing. Was this the golden cup of victory that he thought was going to be so sweet to taste?

Daddy looked at the storekeeper. He just had to have a piano. That was his whole existence, his reason for being.

The storekeeper met his gaze with an icy stare. "If you'll excuse me, I've got to get back to my figures. My clerk made a five-cent error and I've got to trace down the mistake."

Daddy clenched his fist in his coat pocket. If it wouldn't have ruined his hands, he would have hit the old skinflint. He probably had enough money to buy twenty pianos.

Daddy walked out of the store. He pulled out his watch, his expensive, solid gold, Hamilton railroad watch his Mama had presented to him the night before graduation. She had saved so long to buy this beautiful present. If he could hitch a ride back to the railroad station in LaJara, he might catch the night train back to Provo.

Two more days and nights. Could he weather it? Anything would be better than this dismal, little town. But what would his friends say when he returned? They had given him such a grand farewell. They expected such glorious things of him. They said he was going straight to Broadway. "The most handsome, the most talented, the most likely to succeed" read the sign which his classmates waved in the breeze as "their hero" departed on the little narrow gauge railroad car headed for Colorado. It would be hard to return so soon acknowledging his defeat, his very first try at the big world.

A horse and buggy drew up at the mercantile store, and a young woman alighted from it. With her was a kindly-looking, bearded gentleman. He looked as if he might be her father.

Daddy's heart gave a pulsating thud as a pair of limpid, cornflower blue eyes looked directly at and through him, a feeling he had never before experienced.

"You must be the new music teacher. My father and I drove to LaJara to pick you up. We missed the train since it got in early. I'm so sorry. How on earth did you get to Sanford?" As she looked up at Daddy, she straightened a lock of hair beneath her sailor hat which was perched primly on her head.

"I walked — it wasn't really that far. Besides my legs needed stretching after that long train trip." Daddy wondered if she heard the wild beating of his heart that thundered in his ears.

"I'm Lars Mortensen, and this is my daughter, Pearl." The elderly gentleman greeted Daddy with a warm handshake. "We're surely excited about having a music teacher in these parts. The folks around here are hungry for music. We've never had a full-time music teacher, and we're mighty thrilled about it. In fact, we've taken up a collection for a piano to be brought up from Denver. We'll put it wherever you stay. It's a genuine Baldwin and we hope you'll be pleased with it." He looked up at Daddy with a twinkle in his gentle eyes. He reminded Daddy of a picture of Santa Claus.

"We hope you'll board with us. We've got a big house, it's not fancy or elegant, but I'm the last of twelve children, so we have a few empty rooms," said Pearl eagerly. "Ma is out midwifing a lot of the time and I clerk here at the store of my brother-in-law. He's married to my eldest sister, Laurette. You'll have the house to yourself and you won't bother anyone with your practicing.

Daddy's face flushed with uncontrollable pleasure as he looked down at the beautiful, little Danish girl with the cornflower eyes and Dresden skin. She hardly came up to his shoulder. What a beautiful mother she would make for the daughters he dreamed he would have some day. They would all be as pretty as their mother and would harmonize just like angels. Boys were so clumsy; oh, maybe he would have a couple of them to take on hikes and nature walks. Ah—but the girls—he would teach them to sing and they would be so good they would become famous. Someday their names would be seen in lights, even at the Palace Theatre in New York City! And what would they be called? Oh yes, the famous King Sisters. They would take their name from their father!

Daddy aroused himself out of his dream and looked out over the prairie. The wind had stopped blowing. The sky was a brilliant indigo blue. The horizon was endless; he could see forever.

"Papa, take Mr. Driggs' suitcase and we'll drive him to our house, that is, if Mr. Driggs would be pleased to board with us." Her luminous eyes looked so demure.

Daddy's heart took another somersault. "That's very kind of you. You'll never know how kind," he stammered as he helped Miss Pearl into the buggy and then took a seat beside her. Mr. Mortensen headed down the dusty road lined with wild roses, columbines, sweet peas, and holly hocks. Was there ever such a dazzling, beauteous town as Sanford, Colorado?

Daddy surely could tell a story. We didn't need televisions or radio. It was all there in living color of words around the campfire at night. I don't know whether it was completely factual — I mean the dream he had about having girls — but it certainly influenced us to harmonize and become good at our singing trade. We never wanted to let Daddy and his dream down.

Of course, after the romantic stories, came the singing. That's where we really learned to harmonize, singing together around the glowing embers of the campfire in the scenic mountains of Utah with the summer moon shining down in our faces.

We stayed in those beautiful mountains all summer but one morning we awoke and found ice had formed on the water pail. We knew it was time to head back to Ephraim and Daddy's new school job. What we didn't know at that time was that Mama was adding to our family, a little blonde baby girl to be born in January. We would name her Yvonne. I guess that was the reason Mama was so reluctant to climb those mountain peaks and bathe in cold mountain streams, when her brood followed Daddy's every step.

And now we were back in Ephraim. The furniture had arrived, and everything was going pretty well until the afternoon Alyce and I lost our playhouse.

Our playhouse was the big, wooden crate that the grand piano had been shipped in from Denver. Alyce and I would play there hour after hour. Mama generally knew where she could find us.

Daddy had just come home from school and was sitting at the dining room table reading the morning paper when the big horse-drawn express wagon drew up in front of our house. A man alighted and came to the front door. We heard Daddy talking to the man in a loud, angry voice. And thén Mama joined in and we heard her crying.

Pretty soon another man came to the front door, and shortly after that we saw them wheel the grand piano out of the living room and put it on a dolly and hoist it into the express wagon and drive away.

"Can you believe their taking that piano just because we were delinquent with our payments for three months?" Daddy was saying angrily.

"Oh, King, what are we going to do without that grand piano?" Mama wept.

Daddy walked out the kitchen door. His face was ashen and he looked desperate.

"Luise and Alyce, get out of that piano box and take all your dolls, too," he demanded.

We ran into the kitchen. Suddenly we heard the chopping of wood and we looked out the kitchen window and saw our playhouse turned into a bunch of kindling.

Daddy didn't come home for dinner that night, and Mama's face looked drawn and worried. She put us to bed early.

It was sad to lose our playhouse, but I felt more sorry for Daddy. Another one of his dreams had flopped. How could we sing "Ain't We Got Fun" and "Swinging Down the Lane" without Daddy playing that beautiful, big grand piano? How could he compose those lovely little operettas he had been putting on at the colleges where he taught? The piano was on its way back to Denver — repossessed! The house seemed sad and lonely without it.

When Christmas came to Ephraim, everything was blanketed with snow, and Daddy and big brother Karleton hiked up to the nearby hills and brought home a lovely fresh pine tree. How its glorious fragrance filled the air as it sat waiting to be decorated by Mama and Daddy Christmas Eve. But we were going to learn this Christmas was to be quite different from the ones we had known before. Daddy and Mama were always lavish at Christmas and sent off to Sears and Roebuck catalog for dolls and toys, even if we couldn't afford them. But this Christmas we had seen odd-shaped packages under the bed, and we were very curious about them. We went to bed after steaming baths in the old tin tub which sat in front of the wood stove in the kitchen, and wondered just what Christmas morning had in store for us.

Early in the morning we were awakened by the strains of a Christmas march Daddy had composed. He was playing it on a rented upright piano. As we rushed to get dressed in our best finery (it was a tradition in our house to get dressed up Christmas morning before we saw the tree and toys), we saw Mama rushing around getting out the divinity and sweetmeats she had prepared during the week. Then after a hurried, warm breakfast we got in line from the youngest to the oldest and marched into the little darkened parlor all aglow with that beautiful candle-lit tree. Daddy played the Christmas march as we entered. When we looked under the tree we saw no toys, just musical instruments — a clarinet for Karleton, violins for Maxine and Alyce, an accordian for me, and a drum for Donna. There was a C-melody sax for Daddy and even a cello for Mama. Our disappointment showed but Daddy had decided to have his own family orchestra. That very afternoon, after our big Christmas dinner, Daddy got his family orchestra going and after moans and groans and discordant tones, the Driggs family orchestra was born.

With Daddy's tutelage it didn't take us long to get quite professional, and before we knew it, we were playing every little whistle stop in Utah. We were resplendent in our black and white satin uniforms Mama had made. We recited musical monologues, danced and sang and played our musical instruments. The program was based on the theme of home. We were advertised as a "talented family admirably trained." We were a forerunner to many show business families yet to come.

Of course, we couldn't stay in Utah forever. The towns were too small, the pay the same. Sometimes we would make ten dollars, sometimes more and sometimes less. Sometimes it would be a rooming house we would stay in for the night or if we were feeling flush, Daddy would pop for an auto camp, as we called them in those days. But sometimes, it would be just a haystack that some generous farmer would offer us. We loved it. We were cozy and together, and we would look up at the stars, and Daddy would point out the North Star and the Big Dipper, and we would thrill at the vastness of this universe.

We decided we had to go where the big time was and that meant California. We filled the grub box with homemade bottled chicken and bottles of tomato juice (in case we died of thirst) and headed southwest across that big, unfriendly desert to California. The road was unpaved, full of chuckholes, and very lonely. There were very few gas stations along the way.

What a brave little band we were. Daddy had found a booking agent to get us a few dates along the way to help pay expenses. And so we set out, not a company of wagon trains like our Mormon grandparents, just one little family alone in an old Dodge touring car with boxes of instruments and costumes strapped to the running board, quilts and kids overflowing in the back seat, and two water bags hanging over the engine. California here we come!

But we didn't quite make California. It seems our booker, who went on in advance of us, had disappeared taking with him the money that Daddy had loaned him for expenses. After countless flat tires that Daddy and Karleton had to repair and a hole in the crankcase caused by a boulder in the dusty road, the old Dodge decided to call it quits. We had just crossed the Nellie Bush Ferry at Parker, Arizona, and were headed for Phoenix when it happened. I guess we were just too much for the old car. It was a bit much for Mama, too, because it was here she broke the news to us that she was six months pregnant. We were lucky a truck came along — the driver felt sorry for us and towed us into Phoenix. Daddy had a brother there, and hoped he might help Daddy get a teaching job for the winter.

"In the spring, we start out for California again," Daddy said, "if things go well!"

Things didn't go well in Arizona. Alyce got scarlet fever, and the rest of us got the mumps. Mama was quarantined in one room of the house with Alyce, and it was Christmas again. No snow, no Christmas tree, and Mama couldn't even make Christmas divinity, she couldn't leave Alyce. Things were pretty depressing that Christmas Eve, but during the night as we lay in our beds wondering if Santa would find us in Phoenix, we heard a chopping sound. What could that be?

In the morning, Daddy was cheerful. "Get up kids and get dressed and come down to breakfast. Your French toast is waiting." Then he started playing that familiar Christmas morning march.

We weren't expecting any presents, but he insisted we march into the living room while Alyce and Mama looked forlornly through the glass door that imprisoned them from the rest of the house. But there was a Christmas tree! It was beautifully decorated and lit with glowing candles. But the smell was different somehow. It smelled like a pepper tree, and so it was. Daddy had cut it down and decorated it for Christmas. Later, we learned that the owner of our rented house was not too happy about losing his nice backyard shade tree. The Arizona summers needed all the shade trees they could get.

10

California

In the spring, we headed for California with our new passenger — a baby boy we called Billy. He was to be our caboose after this long train of girls. Daddy always called Karleton, our oldest brother, his faithful little engine.

As we entered the Los Angeles city limits, we looked down the boulevard lined with orange groves and eucalyptus trees. Mama made Daddy stop the car at a filling station. She wanted all of us to change our clothes. It was necessary we be well groomed despite our old touring car, she didn't want us to be mistaken for people from the dust bowl who were streaming into California. Daddy put on his blue serge suit and grey fedora hat and Mother, a black and white satin dress and her black feather hat that she always saved for nice occasions. We girls put on our silk and taffeta dresses that had been made by Aunt Golda before we left Utah. We must have been a funny sight in the old dusty touring car with the grub box and all the paraphernalia on the side. But we had class and we wanted California to know it.

California in 1924 was all we hoped it would be. Orange groves graced the countryside, the air was cool and balmy, and orange juice stands in the shape of an orange were everywhere — you could stop and get all you wanted to drink for a dime. The vegetable and fruit stands were numerous as were the theatres and churches. Daddy told us that 50 million people a week went to see the "It" girl, Clara Bow, "The Sheik," Rudolph Valentino, and Charlie Chaplin, "The Little Tramp." The popular gangster movies, westerns and *The Ten Commandments* were all right here in Hollywood.

Daddy said the motion pictures were responsible for the new morality in the world. Gertrude Stein had labeled this the "lost generation," and there was a lot of talk about the "flaming youth." Women were bobbing their hair, wearing short dresses, using lipstick and smoking cigarettes. Movies may have been responsible for a lot of that but for every theatre there seemed to be a church. Daddy decided that we were going to perform in churches. He would show these Californians what a real musical Mormon family was like. He would do his own booking and not trust anyone else.

Daddy did pretty well with his bookings and before long we had a schedule of family concerts. Our family would arrive at the church where the concert was to be held. Our old Dodge would be bursting with children, musical instruments (which included a trap drum set), costumes of black and white satin or shades of irridescent taffeta, a large paper bag filled with tuna sandwiches, bananas and fig newtons, and a bottle of black shoe polish. Daddy always put a nice, shiny polish on his shoes the last minute before going on stage. And, of course, he would gather his family around him and we would kneel in true Mormon fashion and have family prayer, asking the Lord to bless us so that we would give an excellent performance.

After the concert, we would pack up our belongings, pick up whatever child had fallen asleep on one of the congregation member's lap and pile into the old Dodge. We would be jubilant if the reception and offering were good, dejected if it were poor. But always we would be singing and harmonizing as we made our way home through the balmy and sometimes foggy cold nights of California. Many times we stopped at the big fruit markets, which were run by the Japanese and were the forerunners of the big supermarkets of today. We bought fig jam, honey, and oranges for our little treat when we arrived home.

And so the years rolled by, and we were getting to be young ladies, but the church concerts were not growing the way we were. In fact, we were having a difficult time, and things were a little grim. One summer we headed back to Utah and Idaho to play fairs, which offered better money than the churches did. Our old Dodge had completely worn out, so Daddy felt he had to do something about it. One afternoon just before dinner, we heard a horn tooting. We ran to the window to see who it was, and there was Daddy sitting proudly in a new car. It wasn't really new; it was secondhand, but it was new to us, and it was nifty.

"It's a Graham-Paige," Daddy told us. "It's much roomier than the Dodge and much more comfortable. Wait 'til you ride in it!"

We all piled in, and Daddy let Karleton drive it around the block. Karleton was a better driver than Daddy, and Daddy wanted Karleton's opinion of it. Karleton approved and so did we! It was roomy and luxurious.

"King, how did you pay for it?" Mama was the one person in the family who was concerned about finances. She had to be; Daddy was not.

"I put a $50 down payment on it and we'll pay twenty-five a month 'til it's paid for. It won't be hard with those fairs we've got in Utah and Idaho. It'll be a cinch!"

It wasn't a cinch. We had a few fairs, but not enough to make ends meet. It's best described in Daddy's diary from 1929.

> Tuesday, September 10. Pocatello, Idaho. Our summer engagements in Utah haven't been a financial success. I was looking forward to our Idaho fair dates, hoping they would pull us out of

the red. But during our performance a tragedy occurred which I am loath to record. Scant proceeds in summer put us behind in payments on automobile and instruments. Car reclaimed by detectives and officers and I was detained at Pocatello while legal matters were straightened out, family going ahead without me, filling dates until I am free to rejoin them at Wendall's Corn. Show tour heading to California performance cancelled. Cost us $300.00 attorney fees and car rental.

Wednesday, September 11. Burley, Idaho. Cassia County Fair. Net $120.00 (daytime only). Very difficult to fill this in afternoon and Pocatello same evening under embarrassing circumstances. Feel that we had accomplished the seemingly impossible. We are real troupers and I believe we can do anything fate demands. Laugh, clown, laugh! On with the show.

Friday, September 13. Gooding, Idaho, Schubert Theatre. Vaudeville between pictures for two nights — net $60.00. I was absent from the date. Mrs. Driggs reports very fine reception by manager and standing ovation to return. Made this after very long mileage from Burley Fair and more legal trouble there through lawyer demanding money on instruments and fair refusing to pay salary to anybody but me. She finally collected it, however, and also saved the instruments.

(Mama always was a good talker!)

Monday, September 16. Oakley, Idaho, LDS Recreation Hall, Lyceum concert. Family reports arranging full evening program for the first time without me. Their tears falling on the music the

> while. A midnight picture: family of eight in a rented car — losing their way over the sagebrush prairie — lights of car go out, but they drive on all night from Oakley to Boise, 200 miles, while I was speeding on train in company with detective. Family reunited at attorney general's office, state capitol, where after a brief hearing I was released, extradition refused by Governor. We had only oral permission to take car out of state. Many friends came to our rescue and brother Don C. Driggs wired $150.00 from Phoenix, Arizona.

We finished the rest of our bookings in Idaho and ended up in Twin Falls, where we opened a dancing and music school and resided for the winter. Despite the big Wall Street crash (and our own little private crash), we did pretty well. However, in the spring, we set out for California again.

We were back in Glendale. Glendale wasn't a Hooverville like the Hooverville of New York — a collection of shanties housing unemployed, hungry, people — but we were feeling the pangs of the depression. Maxine was a senior, I was a sophomore and Alyce was a freshman at Glendale High School. We looked quite jaunty in our white, starched middy blouses and navy blue, pleated, serge skirts which reached almost to our ankles. Every girl in the school was required to wear the uniform, and we liked the idea. It kept people from knowing we were quite poor. We had acquired our uniforms at the school gym. They were used and the school sold them to needy children at a very nominal sum.

One afternoon we were coming home from a school assembly and were feeling quite elated. The three of us had sung at the assembly and the kids had loved us and kept us there on stage singing every song we knew — "I Surrender Dear," "Dream a Little Dream of Me," "White Lies" and so on and on. Our sound was new to the kids, a mixture of Bing and the Rhythm Boys and the Boswell Sisters. We were talking excitedly as we walked up the front porch. We had stayed so long at school it was nearly dinner time and the house looked dark and gloomy as we entered it.

"Why don't you get some lights on around here," I yelled, "it looks like a mole's hole!" I flicked the light switch at the door; nothing happened.

Mama was crowded over the fireplace. "Don't bother turning the lights on. It won't do any good. They've been turned off by the power company."

"What is Mama doing at the fireplace?" I thought. It was too warm for a fire. I went over and inspected. Mama was cooking oatmeal and raisins in a big pot. That was to be our supper!

We were humiliated. We knew we were in the midst of a big depression and lots of our friends were having a rough time. But they didn't have to eat oatmeal for supper. We were mortified! We looked at Mama huddled over the fireplace cooking the menial fare. Her body looked swollen and puffy and fat.

"Mama, if we're so poor and we haven't any food, why are you getting so fat?" Alyce just had to get back at Mama for our circumstances. She was right, too. Mama did look fat.

Mama raised herself with an effort and walked right over to Alyce. Lifting her hand, she slapped Alyce right on her mouth. Then with a little sob, she ran into the bedroom and slammed the door.

"Listen, you two," Maxine turned to Alyce and me, her eyes blazing. "You know why Mama is fat? She's pregnant. She's going to have a baby. She was afraid to tell you. She didn't think you would understand. She told me to keep it a secret but if you girls are going to behave like this, I think it's time you knew." Maxine turned and ran into the bedroom to console Mama.

Our sweet, tender, loving Mother had never hit any of us that I could remember. She must have been terribly upset. Alyce and I had been so busy with our friends at school and with our singing and harmonizing, we hadn't noticed Mama's pregnancy and what was really going on at home.

Our concert work had started to slacken. Money was really

tight and the collections at the church concerts were not good. Daddy had pounded the pavement until the soles of his shoes were thin as paper and full of holes, but work was scarce. Daddy had pupils, but they were negligent about paying, always putting him off for some reason or another. Daddy would continue to teach them, money or not. A lot of families came from the dry dust bowls of Kansas and Oklahoma. They were poor as church mice. They wanted a little music in their lives, so Daddy would teach their children with hardly any remuneration. Mothers bringing their talented little darlings to Hollywood would ask Daddy to help them make their children more professional, but seldom paid. Old folks coming out of the eastern cold to warm their bones in the California sunshine had little money to drop in the contribution plates at the church concerts. Then there were all the hucksters and promoters who gave us golden promises that never materialized.

The needs of our family were getting greater. We were growing up. We girls needed silk stockings and the boys wanted to send their white shirts to the laundry. We were becoming aware of the opposite sex and wanted to look as nice as the other kids did.

That night after our oatmeal supper, we did the dishes. It was generally at this time that we sang and harmonized, making our task easier. Tonight we talked. We discussed our plight and tried to think of what we could do to help the family make a living. Mama and Daddy looked so sad at the table tonight. We just had to think of something.

I came up with an idea. Vocal trios were getting popular and were really quite the rage on radio. Bing Crosby, Al Rinker, and Harry Barris had a trio at the Ambassador Coconut Grove. They were the talk of the town. The Mills Brothers were making it big on records. The Brox Sisters were headliners in vaudeville. But the best sound of all was the sound of three sisters, the Boswell Sisters. We loved them, and copied every note they sang. They had their own show on NBC. People said we sounded very much like them. Our blend was good, and we could swing — just ask the kids at school. Maybe if we tried very hard, we could get an audition at one of the radio stations in Los Angeles. Maybe we could get our own show. That certainly would ease Mama's and Daddy's burden!

We had heard that the song publishers were good at helping young artists get a start if they sang their songs. We were aware of song publishers on Hollywood Boulevard. We finally got up enough courage to walk into one of their offices. It was Harms Publishing Company, and Mable and Lucky Wilber were running the office. They listened to us sing and liked us. They gave us tons of music and said we could rehearse in their offices. They were so wonderful to us and so encouraging. They told us that the Boswell Sisters were leaving KGO up in San Francisco. Since most of the radio shows were broadcasting from the Bay area, KGO would be needing a new girls' trio. Would we like to audition for the spot? Would we? Then we really started practicing. We decided to drop out of school for awhile. There was no time for that sort of childlike stuff. There was women's work to do, and we were all set to do it!

We sat at the piano until our bottoms were numb. We plunked out notes on the keyboard. We quarreled over which harmonies sounded better. We listened to records — everything of the Boswells we could get our hands on. Our throats got raw from too much singing, and Daddy cautioned us, but we didn't listen.

When we reached San Francisco, we drove right up to KGO on Sutter Street. Karleton, who was chauffering the car, found a parking lot across from the radio station. Before we got out of the car, we had our usual family prayer, then powdered our noses, combed our hair, and straightened the seams of our silk stockings. But none of these things seemed to help the audition. We found the radio studio to be cold and clinical. The program director sat in the booth and talked to us over the loudspeaker. She was not too friendly, and we were scared to death. We were singing one song with a ukelele accompaniment. A string broke right in the middle of the number. We were terribly embarrassed and really didn't do our best. Our voices were hoarse and we were tense and stiff. Where was our beautiful sister blend? After the audition was finally over, the program director came out of the booth to speak to us.

"You girls have very clever arrangements, but you are not quite ready for network radio. I suggest you go back to school and practice, practice, practice. Come back in a year, and I think you'll be ready," she said in a condescending tone of voice.

"Come back in a year? Sure! Mama can wait a year to have her baby. The gas and light companies will wait a year for money so they can turn on the power. We'll go on a diet of oatmeal for a year. No problem at all," I thought to myself as we mumbled our thanks and choked back the tears.

When we were out on the street again, I looked over at Daddy and the girls. Karleton had hurried away to pick up the car. Their faces were long and sad. I'd have to talk fast to cheer them up—especially Alyce—and Daddy was almost as bad. All our beautiful plans had disintegrated, but we couldn't give up.

"Why don't we go over to KLX in Oakland? You know they wrote us saying we could audition for a job there. It won't be as much money as at KGO because it isn't network, but at least it will be something."

Daddy's face brightened. "Luise is right. It would be ridiculous to give up after the first try. Remember your pioneer heritage — they certainly didn't give up when they were discouraged. Besides, it's a beautiful day for a ferry boat ride to Oakland. It will be relaxing. Just what you need, and I'll bet you girls can get that job at KLX. I never did like women program managers anyway."

We did get the job at KLX in Oakland. We auditioned and they liked us. In fact, they loved us! We were relaxed and for some reason, we never sang better. They hired us for the enormous sum of twenty-five dollars a week.

Now Mama could have her baby in the hospital like other women were doing. All the rest of us had been born at home with the help of Grandma as midwife. The family could move up to Oakland. We'd find a house to rent, and we could support the family in style. It was at KLX that we changed our name from *Driggs* to *King,* taking Daddy's middle name, William King Driggs. *Driggs* just was not theatrical enough. Anyway, it brought us luck, and we were soon offered a job for fifty dollars a week at the large, powerful radio station, KSL in Salt Lake City, Utah. That's where Horace Heidt heard us and sent us the telegram that was to change our lives—especially Mama's.

It was hard for her to see her little birds fly away from their nest, even though the nest had been a broken down, old touring car. But it had been feathered with a lot of love, work, and need for each other. It was hard for her and Daddy to see their girls go out in that teeming jungle called "the world." But they had prepared us well. With tears streaming down our faces and many warnings about the evils of life, we left our nest and headed for the big metropolis of San Francisco to begin our lives with the big bands.

11

The War

As our lives with the big bands continued, so did the big war. We heard it on the radio, we read it in the newspapers, and Daddy, ever the school teacher, kept us pretty well informed.

At first, the war in Europe only brought us a lot of great songs to sing, "I Don't Want to Walk Without You, Baby," and "The White Cliffs of Dover." These were tear-jerker songs and we sang them with feeling and people loved them.

It was with the Selective Service Training Act that the world around us became more than music and song. All male citizens up to the age of thirty-five inclusive had to register for the draft. This meant we could start losing some of the boys in our band — and those side men were mighty important.

There was much competition in the band business, much like the sports field of today. There was a lot of swapping of side men. The bands tried to do everything they could to enhance their popularity. They each tried to develop a distinctive style which would attract attention and sell records. Tommy Dorsey played high trombone and slowed his ballads way down. Artie Shaw piped away on his clarinet with a Jewish-like chant. Glen Miller voiced his sax section like a big-sounding pipe organ. Some leaders blew through straws in a glass of water and some even made the effect of blowing bubbles as they went on the air.

Certainly not all of the bands were swing bands; the sweet bands were popular as well. Topping that list was Guy Lombardo, followed closely by Kay Kyser, Sammy Kaye, Jan Garber, Blue Barren, Art Kassel, and Shep Fields. Lawrence Welk was around, but he really hadn't developed his career yet.

In 1942 one of the dance polls listed the bands in order of popularity: Glen Miller, Harry James, Tommy Dorsey, Jimmie Dorsey, Vaughn Monroe, Alvino Rey, Benny Goodman, Woody Herman, Kay Kyser, Charlie Spivak, Sammy Kaye, Claude Thornhill, Gene Krupa, Count Basie, Artie Shaw, Charlie Barnet, Johnnie Long, Freddy Martin, Guy Lombardo, and Hal McIntyre.

Despite the fear of the draft, the band business was riding high. We were on the road constantly. We made several trips to Hollywood to do pictures and also to play the Paladium. It was "the" thing for bands to appear in pictures. It stimulated the box office as big bands and their singers were the number one item in show business. The thoughts of making pictures in Hollywood were terribly exciting, but we found that, in reality, making pictures was a lot of dull, hard work.

Our first picture was with RKO and starred Buddy Ebson and June Haver. It was called *Sing Your Worries Away*. Alvino's band was hired to play, and we were hired to sing.

We would have to get up at four o'clock in the morning when we were working on a picture. It would be dark and foggy and cold. We generally arrived at the studio without having had any breakfast and wearing slacks or some sort of grubby clothes which were needed to keep comfortable on the cold and drafty picture sets.

First we would be sent to the hairdressers who shampooed and set our hair each day. Usually these hairdressers were the best in the business. Then we'd go to the makeup department.

That was always fun. It was relaxing to have them fuss with our faces and the lights felt warm and comfortable. We always came away from there feeling beautiful, but somewhat alike. I think the movie stars of the forties all looked as if they came out of the same mold. They didn't have the individuality today's movie stars have.

Then we would go back to the hairdressers who would finish our hairdos. If our hair happened to be a little thin, they would make it look thicker with falls and wigs and hairpieces. Then they'd put a piece of sheer netting around our hair and we would be off to the dressing room where the wardrobe was waiting.

Having costumes designed by the famous studio designers, Vera West, Irene, and Adrian, was a revelation to us. Everything was fitted into the costume. If one were flat-chested, padding would be added in the right places. If one's hips were too small, more pads. We didn't have trouble in either of those departments. There were bones at the waist to make it look tiny and layers and layers of skirts were used for formal evening wear.

After the picture had finished shooting, we were able to buy, at very reasonable prices, most of the gowns they made for us. We took them home to show Maxine how professionally they were done and she learned much from those wonderful designers at the studios.

A breakfast cart with coffee, tea, milk, orange juice, sweet rolls and doughnuts came around by 9:00 and we were hungry. It seemed by then, we had been up for days and we were just getting to the set.

We thought we were going to go right into our songs, but it wasn't done that way. Hours would pass as lights and sets were arranged. Sometimes it would be four or five in the afternoon before they would get around to shooting us. We would be weary and tired from waiting and our hair and makeup would be somewhat depleted to say the least. We noticed a lot of the movie stars and extras knitting, needlepointing, or reading — anything they could do to relieve the monotony. It was monotonous, and we were amazed at the patience of the stars.

While working on *Sing Your Worries Away* we scarcely sang. When we first got to the studio, we were directed to a rehearsal hall. There were four boy dancers waiting for us. For one solid week we rehearsed dance routines with the four boy dancers whirling us around, lifting us up, doing everything except singing. We were singers, not dancers. Why had the studios hired us? But we found out the studios were good at wasting money.

We also worked at MGM in a picture called *Thrill of A Romance* starring Van Johnson, June Allyson, and Lucille Ball. We met Ava Gardner, a young southern belle who was being groomed for stardom.

We also did pictures for Universal Studios. One was a musical, *Larceny with Music,* starring Allan Jones and Kitty Carlisle. All of the musicals were featuring bands and singers.

We were still amazed at how the studios wasted their money. We would spend weeks and weeks on one little routine and many times it would be cut. We prided ourselves on being fast workers. We were alert and caught on to routines easily. In radio, we found everything was geared to a fast pace with no time for mistakes. Making movies was like working in a factory. It really was quite boring, and we certainly didn't get any immediate reaction from our performances but it was thrilling later to see ourselves on the big screen.

When we went west, we generally had our own train car. The jumps were a little too far apart to do it by bus. Besides, we could afford it. We were finally making money. After about a week on the train, we would sidetrack our car and decide it was time everyone had a good hot bath. We would rent a couple of rooms in the town's best hotel and order twenty-five bath towels — then wait our turn for a lovely hot bath. How divine it would feel! Dorothy Parker once wrote that when the servicemen who were lying in the muddy trenches of Europe were asked what their first preference would be, they said a hot bath. That came before sex, drinks, or food. So it was with our band.

One particular train trip I will not forget. On December 7, 1941, we were somewhere between Washington, D.C. and Detroit. From Washington we would head out to the Coast to make a picture. Alyce, Syd, Alvino and I were sitting in the club car having an afternoon snack.

"These are good crackers. They don't have any salt on them. You know crackers should never have salt on them; it takes away from the taste of the spread." Alvino was giving us his usual lecture on food.

"Don't you love this guava jelly with the cream cheese?" I said. It was the first time I had tried this combination on crackers. Alvino was always introducing us to new taste treats.

"How long will it be before we get to D.C.?" Alyce asked. She wasn't too interested in crackers and cream cheese and guava jelly. She was more concerned about how much time she would have with Syd.

Syd was with us on a three-day pass. He had gone into the service after their marriage, supposedly just for one year. The army had appealed to the young men to enlist for one year, after which they would be released. However, it didn't work out that way. Those young men who enlisted were not discharged until the war was over.

In the club car we had the radio on, enjoying the music while discussing food.

"Alvino, tell me, how did you get to be such an authority on food?" Syd questioned.

"Well, you know I was born in San Francisco and my dad used to take me to all the wonderful restaurants when I was only five years old. He taught me a lot about good food and good fishing. But music, I had to learn by myself," Alvino explained.

"The music on the radio suddenly stopped and a garbled voice was making an announcement. "Turn up the radio, Alvino. I'd like to hear what they're saying," Syd said.

"Ladies and gentlemen, I regret to inform you that at 6:00 a.m. this morning Pearl Harbor was bombed by a fleet of Japanese planes. All military personnel must report immediately to their stations."

"Pearl Harbor bombed! That's impossible. I don't believe it," Alyce said as she looked anxiously at Syd.

"Those damn Japs. I always knew they were a sneaky lot! Well, there goes my three-day pass. I was planning to stay with you until tonight and then get off the train no matter where we were. I could hitch a ride back to Fort Eustice by Monday morning. It looks like we are coming into Washington," Syd said looking out the window.

"We sure are. There's the dome of the Capitol." Alvino pointed to the Washington skyline outside the window.

"Oh, Syd, you don't have to leave now. You can't. You've got a three-day pass!" Alyce's eyes started filling with tears.

"You heard what the announcer said. All military personnel report to their stations immediately. I guess that means me, too."

Syd got up and started walking out of the club car. We all followed. Alyce was sobbing uncontrollably. I put my arms around her. I felt so sorry for her. She was six months pregnant, and I knew what she was thinking. "Would Syd still be around when their baby was born?"

From the moment Syd enlisted, he and Alyce had to grab at any moment they could get, as many other young couples did. It was a weekend marriage, a tumultous, romantic, hectic weekend — an emotional, passionate, short three days. They never knew but what the weekend would be their last time together.

Alyce and Syd had met at the Rustic Cabin. Syd was a handsome college boy. After their marriage while Syd was serving his stint in the army, he sometimes got a weekend pass. Naturally, he would spend his time at the Rustic Cabin where we were playing. We would set up a table, right on the bandstand, so that he could be with Alyce during intermission. Saturday nights at the Rustic Cabin were packed, and in the smoke-filled roadhouse, kids hung from the rafters, making it difficult for Alyce and Syd to have much privacy. We tried to make it easy for them to get together as much as possible. Every moment counted for them.

One particular Saturday night Alyce was depressed as Syd had called to say that his weekend pass was cancelled. Alyce was doing a solo at the mike, a song that Matt Dennis had written, "Everything Happens to Me." I had written some special lyrics at the end, which were appropriate and sentimental and personal for the war years. Matt Dennis' words were:

> I make a date for golf, and you bet your life it rains.
> I try to sing a song, and the guy upstairs complains.
> I guess I'll go through life just catching cold and missing trains.

I added these lines:

> We planned a lovely wedding, and we thought we'd make it May.
> We even called the preacher, and reserved him for that day.
> But just as we were married, Uncle Sam called you away.
> (And then there was a bugle call and Alyce finished the song with)
> Everything happens to me.

As she was singing the song, her eyes teared and all the kids gathered around the mike to watch her. They knew those big blue eyes were going to spill over momentarily, and they wanted to be around to console her. Just as she got to the last line and the trumpet player started playing the bugle call we had interpolated into the arrangement, there was a commotion on the floor. Was someone starting a fight we wondered? It happened a lot when the young people were drinking and dancing and full of emotion. No, it was Syd, resplendant in his army uniform, making his way through the crowded dance floor. He was coming right towards the bandstand and his Alyce. When he got up there and Alyce realized who it was — what an embrace! Romantic? You bet, just like the finish of a

Nelson Eddy/Jeanette McDonald movie. The kids were excited, and cheered and whooped. Then Alvino and the band went into the "Jersey Bounce" and the place started jumping. Everyone was jitterbugging while the band roared.

Syd grabbed Alyce and started jitterbugging. Syd was a good dancer and so was Alyce. The crowd stepped back and let Alyce and Syd have the floor. What a picture they made—Syd in his army uniform and Alyce in her pretty evening gown. The crowd went wild and cheered and stamped their feet and the band kept beating out the rhythm.

As we continued our trip, we sadly watched military men detraining at various points along the way. Our trek to Hollywood to do a picture for RKO had lost a lot of its excitement and glamour. How could Hollywood compete with the big show going on in real life? But the show went on and so did the band.

Those "fabulous forty" years were wonderful years. Even with the big war going on, the tragedies and the heartbreaks, there were happy memories for most of our generation, and big bands were certainly a part of them.

Glen Miller probably left his mark on those years more than any other band leader. His band was tops in records and personal appearances. But right at the peak of his career in 1942, he entered the war. His last engagement before going into the service was at the Central Theatre in Passaic, New Jersey. His fans crowded the theatre and wept as he played his last tune. He entered the service as a captain and later became a major. He formed a fine service band and in 1944 was stationed in England. Glen Miller was headquartered in London, but because of the way London was being blitzed every night it was decided to move the band to New Bedford to do the armed forces broadcast. The very night they moved to New Bedford, the building that had housed the band in London was bombed. Not long after that, Glen was promoted to major, and to celebrate, the band which included Ray McKinley and Johnnie Desmond, had a big party.

The next morning, December 15, the band was planning to

go to Paris to do some in-person shows. The new major decided to fly ahead of the band to find an appropriate spot in which to appear. Although he was in the Air Corps, Glen really didn't care much about flying. The commander in charge, who had his own plane, insisted upon flying Glen across the Channel. He was sort of a hotshot flying ace who thought nothing of taking chances, a show-off in the sky. It was a thick, foggy, soupy morning and all planes had been grounded. But the colonel didn't pay any attention; he didn't even bother to file his flight plan. Against Glen's wishes, the colonel managed to get Glen to fly with him. Three days passed before anyone knew that Major Miller had disappeared. No one really found out what happened. Searchers combed the sea for weeks, but no trace of the plane or either man was found. It was sad to lose Glen especially to carelessness. His death left a vacancy in the hearts of all the kids and all members of the band business—but his music, his style, and "In the Mood" live on to this day.

Artie Shaw was another leader to enter the armed services. Artie joined the navy in 1942, and toured the South Pacific with a fine navy band. Earlier, in 1937, Artie formed a great swing band and made a big hit out of "Begin the Benguine." We sang with him in 1939, and we saw how he was loved, especially by the girls. But Artie couldn't care less. He was an intellectual snob and was always disbanding his band and starting over again. His public didn't mind; they loved his music.

Many of the band leaders, as well as sidemen, had caught the fever and were joining the military. Bob Crosby, Larry Clinton, Ray McKinley, Sam Donahue, and Claude Thornhill were donning service uniforms. Our good and faithful friend, Jack Egan, joined the coast guard along with Hollywood personalities Caesar Romero and Victor Mature.

Everyone was very patriotic and involved. One of our own great sidemen, Dean Kincaid, who made a lot of Tommy Dorsey's and Alvino's hit arrangements, told us what happened when he was in the navy band on the *U.S.S. Franklin.* When the airplane carrier was hit, a lot of the musicians grabbed their instruments and started playing to keep up the spirits of the crew. They played and then laid down their instruments and fought fires and then played some more while the crippled ship battled the Japanese. Five of the musicians were killed, but the music kept on until the *Franklin* claimed victory.

Some of the big band leaders didn't go into the service. Tommy and Jimmie Dorsey, Harry James, and Les Brown did their bit by playing for the USO and at various army and navy bases.

However, with us there was something in the air besides the war and big band music. On June 28, 1943, sister Donna married handsome, dashing Navy Lieutenant J.G. Jim Conkling. Jim was the young, blonde college boy from Maplewood, New Jersey, who had visited the Rustic Cabin and had his eyes on our Donna. Jim, now a graduate of Dartmouth, had courted Donna with cute notes, clever games, and various other ways to gain her attention. He would show up at the Earl Theatre in Philadelphia, the Paramount Theatre in New York, or the Meadowbrook in Cedar Grove, New Jersey, always with a surprise for Donna. Jim had a keen mind and a lot of creativity and would become an important figure in the music world, but at the time of their marriage, he was a naval officer who looked dashing in his crisp military whites. They were to be married at our beautiful home in Encino, California. Alvino and I had purchased the home from movie director Buddy de Sylva for the exorbitant price of $17,500. The yard had a wishing well, a horse ring and stables—and—a sixty foot living room. It was Hollywood glamour at its best and a lovely setting for a wedding.

Jim's mother was coming out via train. During the war, the trains were inevitably delayed and her train was six hours late. Could the wedding guests wait six hours or should the ceremony be performed without Mrs. Conkling? The bride and groom couldn't make the decision so Alvino did. We would wait for Mrs. Conkling. What would the wedding be without the groom's mother? Alvino seemed to sense what was really important in life and knew how to make a fast decision while the rest of us were still debating the question.

We had hired a young jazz musician, Dave Barbour, and his trio to play at the wedding and they kept the guests entertained during the long wait. He had brought along his young wife, Peggy Lee, who was just beginning to make a stir in Hollywood with her sexy voice. She and I sat in the kitchen and compared notes about life on the road. Peggy had just left Benny Goodman.

Mama Conkling finally arrived and the wedding went on. Donna was the last of the four King Sisters to marry, and we were beginning to realize that soon we might end our singing careers and start others as young wives and mothers. But we combined those careers and went on and on!

It was also in 1943 that Alvino decided to go into the service. The band was doing so well, both financially and musically, that it was hard for us to break it up.

But it was almost impossible to keep a band together. There was a feeling of unrest in the air. No one could really settle down to anything as long as that war was going on but our band kept playing despite the constant changes in personnel. We were traveling and working harder than we had ever done. The band was playing better, and we had some fine musicians like Nick Fatool and Ralph Muzzilla with us and some effective swing arrangements by Billy May.

Another deterrent to the success of the bands was the recording strike which banned musicians from making records. We sisters made a few records by ourselves, without any musicians—just a bass singer going "oom-pah." They sold well, but we hated them. We needed the big band.

So in 1943 Alvino made the decision to break up his band and join the navy. What a sad day it was when I went with him to the old Union Depot on Los Angeles Street and said goodbye to him. I wasn't sure when or where I was going to see him again.

We had driven down to the train station in my new, blue Ford convertible Alvino had given me for an anniversary present. It was the first car I had ever owned and I loved it. It was fun driving around the valley with the top down, inhaling the fresh, unsmoggy air and soaking up the California sunshine that was prevalent then. Life had been so good to us the past year. We were enjoying our beautiful Encino home as well as keeping up with our music. Alvino had played at the Casino Gardens in Ocean Park with his band and worked the graveyard shift at Lockheed. We sisters had been singing on the "Ozzie and Harriet" radio show. We were terribly busy, yet we were loving the country life of the San Fernando Valley. But as we were driving to the station, it hit me that all this was coming to an end.

I clung to Alvino's arm as we made the long walk through the station to the train. I looked around at the grand, old Union Pacific station with its beautiful tile floors and arched windows. It was generally rather empty. But that day it was filled with girls and boys having to say goodbye—most of the girls were crying and the boys were looking wretched. Mothers and fathers and families were there, gathered around their boys, sniffling and sobbing and carrying on. What a forlorn picture. The only thing I could console myself with was that I was not alone. We were all in it together, that was a little comfort to me, but not much.

Alvino carried a small suitcase that held a change of clothes and a few toilet articles. He didn't need much as he would be issued his naval attire when he arrived at the naval station in Chicago.

We had worked and lived and loved together for so many years. How could we possibly be separated? We had been married six years and he meant everything to me. He was my playmate and friend. I liked him intensely as well as loving him. We had gone fishing and camping together. We both loved the out-of-doors and our musical tastes were the same. I could sit up all night when Alvino joined a jam session and love every minute of it. The warm, happy hours we had spent cooking in the kitchen were a big part of our lives. What was I going to do without him? Alyce had a cute, little baby boy to keep her company. Yvonne was soon to have a baby girl and so was Donna. For some reason, I hadn't become pregnant. We wanted children, but the Lord hadn't willed it so as yet. My life was completely wrapped up in Alvino. How could I go home to that big empty house in Encino and live there with his folks? They had moved there to take care of it while we were on the road.

The thoughts of living in that house without him completely depressed me. I was supposed to be the Pollyanna of the family, but all I could feel was dark gloom in my future. This terrible war was taking my sunshine away.

"There's a coffee stand. Maybe we'll have time to get a little breakfast," Alvino said as we hurried inside and sat down on stools at the counter.

"Your last civilian food. You better enjoy it," I said sadly.

"Well, they say that navy food is better than army chow, anyway," Alvino cheerfully responded.

I wasn't hungry and I certainly didn't feel cheerful. We didn't get a chance to order. We were interrupted by a loud, officious voice coming over a rasping loudspeaker.

"All naval personnel report immediately to car 64 on Track 7."

"That's me, I guess we won't have time to eat. Come on sweetheart, we better hurry."

I had a hard time keeping up with Alvino's long legs as we hurried to Track 7.

We saw all the boys boarding the train, clinging to their girl friends, wives, or families.

Well, this was it. Alvino and I were actually saying goodbye. I had held back my tears until then, but the realization finally struck me. The tears streamed down my face. Maybe I'll never see him again. I just couldn't go on living. Maybe I shouldn't have loved so hard. Maybe I should have spread my affection around like a lot of girls did, then I wouldn't feel so bad. It wasn't fair — this whole damn war wasn't fair!

"Goodbye darling, I love you. I'll write you every night."

"I'll write you, too, but where will I write? I don't even know where you're going."

"I'll let you know. Please don't cry like that, you make it hard for me."

A final kiss and he disappeared into the car. He was lost in an army of guys. I couldn't even wave to him.

"Dear God, don't let anything happen to him. Please bring him home to me safely," I prayed fervently.

I walked back through the train station to my empty blue convertible. I drove down Wilshire Boulevard and then out to the valley on Ventura Boulevard. I took the longest way home I could possibly think of, anything to delay going home to that empty house in Encino.

When I got home I went to our room and lay on the bed and sobbed. After crying until I was drained of tears, I turned the radio on, hoping the music would cheer me up. It didn't. "Saturday Night is the Lonliest Night in the Week" blared out. I flicked to another station:

> I'll be seeing you, in every lovely summer's day,
> In everything that's light and gay.
> I'll always think of you that way,
> I'll see you in the morning sun,
> And when the night is new.
> I'll be looking at the moon,
> But I'll be seeing you.

I sobbed some more and turned to another station — "Don't sit under the apple tree with anyone else but me." The Andrew Sisters and we had both recorded that tune. It sold a lot of records — but now it finally reached home to me.

I didn't hear from Alvino for two weeks, the longest two weeks of my life. I finally got a letter.

Sunday Morning

My Dear Sweet Weezie,

Well, it's started. I still can't believe I'm in the

service. I miss my baby and hated to leave you alone at the train station. It was so sudden. I had planned on a few hours downtown with you, but it was squelched in a hurry, as you know.

We were promptly stuck on a troop train, or should I say cattle car — a sort of barracks on wheels — very rough riding. We didn't get anything to eat until the next morning (oh yes, no club car on a troop train). It seems that most of these fellows (all sailors and marines) have never travelled or been out of the state before and were very anxious to see the country. They were all eyes, glaring out the doors and windows the entire trip. On all our stops we would pile out and get free doughnuts and coffee at the USO. It seemed so funny to me to go up and get a free "hand out."

The trip was monotonous from a view of the countryside, as we had to go all the way to El Paso and then cut up through Oklahoma and Iowa into Chicago. Rain and snow all the way.

Old Chicago looked just the same — dirty and ugly — until we got to the Great Lakes. The buildings and equipment are quite nice. We had to go through the routine of signing up and all that. We were assigned to our company and then sent to bed.

When we got to our barracks, we didn't get to go to bed. It seemed one of the guys sassed the lieutenant and so our whole company had to sandpaper the floor around our bunks. So it was almost midnight before we finally "hit the sack." I know now I'm in the Navy!

I haven't received any instructions as yet, so I can't tell you any plans until I get some information.

I do know I miss you and love you terribly. I'm so lost without you by my side. Please write me everyday to keep me from going "nuts" and I'll do the same.

I love you always and forever,
Alvino

P.S. My address will be:
Alvin Henry McBurney S/lc USNR Co. #846
U.S. Naval Training Station
Great Lakes, Illinois

(Alvino had to use his real name as we didn't have it officially changed until our first son was born.)

I went to see him while he was stationed at the navy pier in Chicago for a short while — what a change! His long, thick, dark hair had all been shaved off for boot camp. He was wearing one of those ridiculous sailor suits. No more beautiful gabardine suits tailored by Jonah that he had worn when fronting the band. It was Saturday night so we decided to go to a movie. We stood in line for hours trying to get into the Chicago Theatre. No one recognized him. A few months before, there had been a long line waiting to get in to see Alvino Rey, his band, and the King Sisters. Our fans had been gathered around the stage door. We'd had a hard time getting away from them to go out to dinner. That week we had broken all attendance records at the Chicago Theatre. Another change!

While the boys were out there fighting, the King Sisters were kept very busy playing army camps and naval bases. We also appeared on many radio shows. "The Maxwell House Show" with Meredith Willson, "The Kay Kyser Musical Kollege" with Phil Harris, and "The Ozzie and Harriet Show" were just a few of them. We kept busy, hoping to make the time without our husbands seem less lonesome and to make it go faster. It helped only a little.

April 12, 1945, Roosevelt was dead. We couldn't believe it;

we were heartbroken by his death along with millions of other Americans. Roosevelt had been good to us. We had felt the depression keenly when we were children in the twenties. When he was elected in 1932, things began looking up for us. Our steady job with Horace Heidt was probably the reason, but we gave Roosevelt part of the credit. He had been good to Daddy, also. Through Roosevelt came the WPA Federal Arts Project which came to the aid of hungry artists. Daddy had been pretty hungry in his life and he was a great artist, we felt. It was because of Roosevelt that Daddy was leading a beautiful choir in Oakland. He also had time to compose a wonderful cantata based on the Book of Mormon and was finding time to do oil paintings — glorious outdoor scenes of the West that he loved so much. WPA was paying artists regularly to do the things they did best.

Then it was August 14, 1945, and the war was over.

12

The Aftermath

The war was over and so was the band business, but the boys didn't know it at that time. They came home from the front, eager to forget their guns and pick up their trumpets and saxophones. They wanted to forget their grim and sordid memories, their tragic experiences, the loss of their buddies. They weren't too crazy about rehashing those war days. They wanted to play that happy music and recapture those romantic pre-war days with "The Summer of Forty-Two" and "All that Jazz." But it wasn't going to be. Those happy, lighthearted kids that played and toured the country with the big bands, had grown up; they were grown now with families and responsibilities. They were grim and saddened by the war and they would never be the same. The country wasn't the same either. Those fabulous years were gone.

The guys found that while they were gone, somebody else had taken their places. A lot of 4-F's were running the music business. They found that operating a band wasn't as easy as it once was. Musicians were demanding big salaries. They weren't playing for kicks any more and they wanted to make up for the time they lost while in the service. And — they learned that people had forgotten how to dance. A new generation didn't even care for that pretty, swingy, romantic dance music. They discovered during the next fifteen years, a thing called Rock and Roll and they had a new idol who swayed his hips and went through all kinds of sexual gyrations.

And so the boys, fresh from the war, tried to pick up their lives where they had left them. The band leaders who had been in the war formed bands again and tried to make it on the road, but it wasn't the same. A lot of the big dance halls had closed down and the kids didn't seem to want to go to those that remained. It was tough to get guys to go on the road again. They wanted to stay home after being away from their families so long.

Some of the musicians decided to settle in Los Angeles and become studio musicians. It was a good life, a good place to raise their families. In the San Fernando Valley, for a few thousand dollars, a musician could have a little house with a nice lawn and garden and even a swimming pool. There would be no more dirty New York apartments with no place for the kids to play. Walking down Ventura Boulevard, one would run into a lot of New York buddies, musician friends and song pluggers, too. It seemed that Broadway had moved to the San Fernando Valley.

Alvino tried it on the road for awhile with a big, swinging band. But it just didn't make it as it had in the early forties. He finally cut down to a small group and played little clubs that were popping up to replace the big dance halls.

With our husbands all home from the war, the King Sisters decided it was time to quit show business and go about the business of raising families. But so far there was nothing for me to raise but little guitars. Alvino and I had been married for nine years and didn't have any babies to show for it. The rest of my sisters were beginning to feel sorry for me. Alyce had her little boy, and Yvonne and Donna both had darling little girls. Alvino and I had been on a nine-year honeymoon and were blissfully happy just with each other but a baby would be wonderful. We finally went to a doctor to see if something was wrong with me or Alvino. The doctor laughed at me after my examination.

"The only thing wrong with you is that you are pregnant."

It had finally happened after nine long years. We had a beautiful baby boy we called Rob. And soon we had a baby girl we named Liza, after Judy Garland's Liza Minnelli and also two grandmothers named Eliza. Several years later we had another baby boy, Jon.

Alyce had two boys and would have three after her second marriage. Yvonne had two beautiful daughters and Donna was to have five children, four girls and a boy. Donna had now moved to New York where her husband, Jim, was president of Columbia Records. Alyce's husband, Syd, rejoined his father in the shipping business in New York, so they also were living in the East.

One day Syd came home from the office with severe pains. The doctor who had been called pronounced it indigestion, but before the night was through Syd had died of a coronary inclusion. It was the first real tragedy in our lives and touched us deeply. Syd was loved by all of us.

Alyce didn't stay east after that. She returned with her two little boys to the West Coast — to the loving strength of our big family.

That's when we decided to go back to work. We replaced Donna with "Baby" Marilyn. She was quite an asset to the group, having had plenty of experience subbing for each of us whenever a new baby was born. We managed to get a new record contract with Capitol Records and with our good friend Lee Gillette acting as our producer, we came up with a new style and sound that attracted some attention. We lowered the keys of our songs and did a lot of low unison, pronouncing our words with distinct articulation. We recorded a new album called "Imagination" and received much acclaim from musicians and music critics. We earned the NARAS award for it in the fifties. With the success of that album, a music panel of judges which included Henry Mancini, Elmer Bernstein, Nelson Riddle, and Percy Faith, voted us as one of the all time greats of popular music along with Frank Sinatra and Ella Fitzgerald. We were listed in *Playboy* magazine as the most promising "up and coming new group One." So now we were really back into show business, playing all the big night clubs of the country.

During our engagement at the Copacabana in New York, we received this write up in *The Cue.*

After Dark
"It's Spring Again"

> I never thought the day would arrive when I'd contemplate sending champagne to a nightclub owner, but just such an impulsive notion is rolling around inside my noggin this fine day. The recipient of the bubbly, if my mood holds, will be Jules Podell of the Copacabana.
>
> Actually, if I order the champagne, I'm going to have to send enough for five, Mr. Podell and the King Sisters, a brace of young ladies who sing in unison (and very well, too!) at that palm-dotted cellar nitery. My reason may seem unimportant to you, but it's *tres* important to me. I've been rejuvenated; I'm a boy again, and just when I was thinking of consulting Gaylord Hauser, too!
>
> You see, the grey hairs have been coming in like mad of recent, and I've been allowing those troublemakers who say "You! Doing a Mambo! Sit down, you're not a kid anymore," and similar jazz to get under my skin, I'd begun to believe them, and if it hadn't been for Mr. Podell and the King Sisters, I'd be well into middle age, instead of being a bright-eyed, quick-stepping youth of 34.
>
> The moment the four King Sisters stepped into the spotlight and began to sing, I thought of another

group of vocalists whom I used to enjoy when I was a young buck. They were called the King Sisters, too, and they worked for a guitar strumming band leader with the improbable name of Alvino Rey. They were mighty big in those days, which was some 12 or 14 years ago. Their big records, if my memory doesn't falter, were "I'll Get By" and "Idaho" and I seem to remember a little gem called "San Fernando Valley."

Well, you could have knocked me over with a swizzle stick when Mr. Podell informed me that this youthful quartet of blonde beauties, currently featured at the Copacabana along with Dennis Day and the orchid-tressed Copa Girls (honest, orchid!) are the self-same King Sisters of my youth! Now, don't get the idea that these kids are cronies. They're beautiful and talented and young — and if they're young, well, so am I, and I feel just great!

Any number of performers who appear in nightclubs hereabouts will be overwhelmed with joy to hear that my mood has improved, my step is bouncier, my reactions are much more optimistic, and — well, I have to go now. Have to deliver a magnum of Piper-Heidsiek to the Copacabana. I was going to send for a messenger, but I've decided to carry it uptown, myself. In fact, I think I'll run the entire way.

Wonder what ever happened to Alvino Rey and his Big Band?

Tim Tayler
The Cue
January 19, 1955

We were enjoying our new career and so were our families. We were playing Vegas and Tahoe. We dragged our kids everywhere with us and they loved it. When we would talk of retiring, our kids wouldn't stand for it. "What, and not go to Tahoe any more, no way!" We always mixed business with pleasure, just as our father had, and it worked for us, too.

And then another exciting opportunity opened for us, our own television show — "The King Family Show."

The show came into being because Yvonne had invited the whole family up to Orinda, California, to do a fund-raising program for her local Mormon congregation. We sisters were all active in the Mormon Church now. Donna was president of the Relief Society, the organization for women; Alyce and I were both involved with the youth organization. Maxine led the choir in her ward and Marilyn was working with the organization for children. We hadn't been that active in church affairs when we were on the road but we all had deep convictions. Mormonism was so deeply instilled in our hearts as young girls, there was never much likelihood of any of us breaking away.

Daddy was leading the choir in a Mormon congregation in Van Nuys and Karleton played the organ. Daddy also had the pleasure of seeing a Book of Mormon cantata that he had composed presented in the famous Mormon tabernacle in Salt Lake City. All of his children sang in his cantata.

It occurred to Yvonne that if we could all sing together in church, why couldn't the King Family appear in concert? The whole family, which was ever increasing in size, had never really performed together professionally. The King Sisters, naturally, and Alvino Rey had performed together for years, but not the great big King family that was growing by leaps and bounds.

We had always sung a lot — on picnics, family gatherings, campouts — there was an abundance of singing and harmonizing. It was generally started by Daddy, who had a nice, big bass voice, and then Mama would chime in with her warm alto voice, and then each of us would find a note to harmonize with, and pretty soon we would have a family choir. Now all the children were beginning to sing and harmonize and to show talent.

It was Vonnie's idea to put on a benefit show with our family choir, the King Sisters, and Alvino Rey and call it the King Family Show.

We all went up to Orinda, some of the kids a little grudgingly because they had basketball games and personal commitments but they went anyway. We rehearsed and rehearsed, and Yvonne finally thought we were good enough to put on a performance.

The show went well, and a lot of people couldn't believe one family could provide such a night of entertainment. There was one man particularly impressed. He was an account executive from ABC. He came backstage after the concert and asked us if we could make a tape of the show to send to his network.

Daddy suggested we do a concert to raise money for his old alma mater, Brigham Young University. We put on a show there which the university taped. ABC saw it and thought we had a winner. They gave us a contract and soon we were being televised nationally as "the first family of television — the King Family."

It was an exciting time for the family which included not only the King Sisters and Alvino, but all the brothers and sisters and their husbands and wives and all the children. It was especially thrilling for Daddy and Mama. At last Daddy's dream had been realized. We were playing the Palace, not the Palace in New York City, but the Palace in Hollywood, California, where our show was taped.

That's where we really learned what hard work was all about. The family was together morning, noon, and night rehearsing, recording, singing, dancing. Whatever the script called for, we did. We developed a different show each week, sort of like learning a complete new musical comedy weekly. This all took place in the sixties, during the period when so many families were having such problems with their kids, and sometimes people thought we were about to lose an entire generation with the hippy movement and drug scene.

Our kids didn't have enough time to get in to much trouble. We were up each morning of the week making arrangements, learning dance routines, studying the script, getting costumes fitted, and learning our songs. We were all in it together from the one-year-olds to Granddad and Grandma in their seventies.

On the family television show in 1964, we celebrated the silver anniversary of the Alvino Rey Band. In the audience sat a handsome grey-haired man. Alvino asked him to come up to the stage and request his favorite number.

"How about Tiger Rag?" There was mischief in his voice.

"You want to get us kicked off the air?" Alvino looked into the cheerful countenance of Stu Woodruff. Stu was the one responsible for getting us fired at the Biltmore.

They gave each other a big bear hug as the studio band went into "Tiger Rag." Stu was still the faithful fan and friend who had remained loyal to us for over 25 years.

One Friday night we were sitting in the audience doing our pre-recording for the show the next day. It was nearly midnight and everyone was getting tired. Grandma and the little ones had been excused earlier but Grandpa lingered. I sat down beside him.

"Daddy, they've finished all the family numbers. Don't you think you should go home? I'll call a cab. We've got a hard day tomorrow."

The girl cousins, headed by Tina Cole, were singing a current tune, "Downtown."

"I want to hear this tune. I like it, it has good rhythm and chord structure. Besides I like to watch my beautiful granddaughters. I'll leave right after they finish."

Daddy was enjoying ever minute of it. He had taught his own daughters to sing "Ah, Sweet Mystery of Life" in pear-shaped tones. But he didn't object to the kids' music of the day. He also seemed to want to cling to every moment. He was afraid he might miss something. Perhaps he felt his time was getting short, and it was.

The next day while he was leading his family in our sign-off signature song, "Love at Home," he suffered a stroke. We rushed him into the dressing room, and while waiting for the ambulance, we had a family prayer, including Sol Illson, our producer and Nick Vanoff, our executive producer. It was funny how they always wanted to be a part of our Mormon prayers, even though they were not Mormon. If they were making a trip to New York to make a business deal, they would ask us to say a prayer for them. I guess they thought we had a hot line to heaven or maybe it was the strength of our family all praying for the same thing.

When the ambulance arrived to take Daddy to St. Joseph's Hospital in Burbank, it was sweet, kind Maxine, our "Florence Nightingale," who sat in the back with his head in her lap.

It was so sad to lose Daddy just as the show was doing so well. But he was seventy-six years old, and he had lived a wonderful, exciting life and died doing what he loved best and with his family all around him enjoying the rewards of his many years of dreaming, teaching, and loving.

> As we were going to press, the sad news reached us that William King Driggs, the father of the King Family and principle subject of this article, passed away, Tuesday, April 6, 1965, following a stroke. In honor of him and his convictions, we are publishing this article with no changes.
>
> "Like a king he stands—tall before his family and the eyes of the nation" in memory as in life.
>
> We extend heartfelt sympathy to his family and friends.
>
> Lorin F. Wheelwright
> *The Instructor*

Mama didn't have such a grand exit. She died in a rest home in Van Nuys, California. I remember the last time I went to see her.

We had been very busy doing our monthly TV specials. She needed so much care that we had to put her in a home. I recall driving down Van Nuys Boulevard. The traffic was thick and I was impatient with it. I was in a hurry to get back to the studio for a production meeting. Then I remembered the doughnut shop and made a quick turn to get to it. I got out of the car and entered the shop. The clerk was not in a hurry. He looked up and recognized me.

"Hello, Miss King. I saw your show last Saturday. I sure did like it. You know, that's my kind of music and my kind of songs. I can't stand that 'kid stuff' you hear nowadays. It's so loud and noisy it drives me crazy! Now, your kids, they're different. They actually seem to like their folks. And all those cute little kids, I don't know how you train them."

He was a friendly soul, pushing sixty, and obviously not in harmony with the young rock world.

"It's not easy," I replied. "We sometimes wish they were midgets!"

We both laughed and I paid him for the doughnuts. He wanted to talk more, impressed by anyone who was a celebrity.

"Your mama sure must like doughnuts. Your brother was in here yesterday buying her some chocolate ones. That's her favorite."

"Yes, I guess she's pretty hooked on them," I said, embarrassed.

Every time we came to see her she asked us for chocolate doughnuts. What made her so concerned about them? What had happened to her mind? I guess the crazy, gypsy life with the hardships, heartaches, the insecurity: the summer camp-out in the Ephraim mountains with no conveniences whatsoever, and a pregnancy she was afraid to share with us — all magic to us but hard on Mama; the tedious trip across the Arizona desert with the old car breaking down momentarily and the fear and danger of the open road, and again another unwanted pregnancy; the countless letters coming to our home, mostly bills with no way to pay them; the arrest of Daddy in Idaho and the family going on without him; the fawning love-sick choir ladies always flirting with handsome, talented King and ignoring her; and finally the "change-of-life baby" she was so embarrassed about. These things had taken their toll and caused her to withdraw from life. It was too bad because the things she worried about turned into blessings — eight beautiful blessings and now she could be so terribly proud.

"Your father and mother must be awfully proud. They've got a wonderful family. It's unusual these days. It seems like everyone is having so much trouble with their kids. We'll be watching your next show; we always watch it. We wouldn't miss it for the world," he continued as he handed me the change.

I picked up the doughnuts, thanked him, and made a hurried exit.

I got back in the car feeling depressed as I drove into the Van Nuys Manor Rest Home. It always made me emotionally upset to go there, to see the frail figures in wheelchairs, to watch pitiful, old people walking aimlessly about, making weird sounds, asking for help. In the sitting room I saw Mama, old and frail, sitting in front of the TV set. There was no picture on it, but she kept staring at it. There was a certain proud beauty about her which I always felt. But her lovely eyes were vacant and staring as she saw me.

"Did you bring me my doughnuts? No one ever brings me doughnuts any more. No one ever comes to see me. The only time I get to see my family is when they are on television. No one loves me!" She took a tissue out of a box by her chair and started crying.

"Mama, that isn't so. You know we all love you. Billy was here yesterday and so was Karleton. You know how busy we are but someone comes here everyday."

Mama was being difficult and it was hard on me.

She continued crying. "They won't let me have anything here, not even my chocolate doughnuts. They won't even let me watch television. They say it disturbs everyone. They don't even want me to watch my own family on television. They don't believe it's my family, no matter what I say."

"Don't cry, Mama, please. It upsets me so. I'm going to talk to the head nurse and insist that they turn on the television for you. In fact, it should be turned on right now because "The

King Family Show" will be coming on in a few minutes. It's a re-run. I can't stay and watch it with you. I've got to rush back to the studio for a meeting. Soon as you get one show taped, you have to plan another. You know how it is. Besides, Billy will be here this evening." I turned on the TV, straightened her shawl, and kissed her sweet, frail cheek. It was so hard to see her this way. I wanted to get away.

Suddenly a picture came on the TV screen. A handsome family with husbands and wives and countless children and grandchildren all dressed alike in evening attire, were singing their theme song, "Love at Home."

"ABC presents the first family of television, the famous King Family."

Mama drew herself up proudly in her wheelchair and said, "Now, they're all here." And then she started singing that old, sweet lullaby that she always sang to us when we were babies.

> Go to sleep, my baby,
> Close your sleepy eyes.
> The lady moon is watching
> Through out the dark blue skies.
> The little stars are peeping
> To see if you are sleeping.
> Go to sleep, my baby,
> Close your sleepy eyes.

As I tiptoed away from Mama that day, I knew she was happy. She was always happy when she sang that song.

I remember her singing that lullaby to us on the train coming into Ephraim way back in the twenties. Mama had just gotten the babies to sleep and suddenly the train gave a lurch and stopped.

"Ephraim, Utah. Anybody out at Ephraim?"

"Children, children, wake up. We have to get off here. This is where we are going to meet Daddy. My goodness, just when I get the baby to sleep."

We gathered up our clumsy bundles and stumbled off the

train, while Mama still hummed that lullaby to the baby, so that it wouldn't wake up.

I never saw Mama alive again. She died the next day and we laid her to rest next to her King in the peaceful Forest Lawn Cemetery in the Hollywood Hills.

13

Encore

Those poignant years of our childhood are gone and those fabulous forties are also gone, and we sisters, with the exception of Marilyn are all doting grandmothers, and loving every minute of it. I'm still married to Alvino. Has it been 45 years? Donna is still married to Jim Conkling, who for some time headed the Voice of America, appointed by Ronald Reagan. Alyce is married to Robert Clarke, a well-known film actor in Hollywood. It was hard to marry again after Syd's death, but Bob, with his sweet, kindly spirit, has made her very happy. Vonnie's Buddy Cole has passed away, and she is now happily married to William Burch, vice-president of MCA. Marilyn lost her young husband, Kent Larsen, a really fine jazz trombonist who sang and played with Stan Kenton. Maxine is still married to her LaVarn. Karleton, after 30 years of marriage was divorced from Hazel, who found him too serious. He married a sweet woman by the name of Jean Ramsey but Karleton died of cancer in the spring of 1982 — the first of the children to go. Bill, a successful commercial artist and married to Phyllis Thayne, died of cancer in the fall of 1982. All the husbands joined the Mormon Church, with the exception of Kent. Daddy never gave up and continued to write long epistles to each of them. His treatises were much too deep for most of them to appreciate. His religious philosophy was much like his political philosophy —heavy! Daddy's writings may have had an influence on our husband's conversions, but I think they were influenced more by seeing our religion being lived day by day and the love and joy of wholesome family life it engendered.

It took a lot of years for us to bring Alvino into the Church. I had made a decision when I married him that I was never going to push him. I didn't want to risk spoiling the sweetness of our relationship. It wasn't Daddy, but our son Rob, who finally got him to join.

When Rob was nineteen, he ceased his church activities and joined the navy. While at sea, a changed spirit came over him and he was reconverted. When he came home, he was most enthusiastic about his faith and approached Alvino.

"Dad, when are you going to join the Church?"

Alvino replied, "How about tonight? You're the first person to ask me. I've been ready for a long time." So Alvino was baptized that very night and we were overjoyed to at long last have him in our fold.

Our three children are following in our footsteps. Rob, the eldest, plays bass; Liza, our beautiful daughter, has been blessed with Alvino's marvelous talent. She plays jazz and swing harp as well as classical, and sings in an individualistic style. We think she will make a mark in the musical world. Jon, our youngest, plays the flute.

Those exciting days of doing the King Family TV Show are also gone. After nearly eight years on the air, the show went off like so many musicals do. We'd had our share of fans, but a lot of young people didn't "dig it." Our teeth were too white, our eyes too blue. We looked too happy. We loved our kids and our kids loved us. It wasn't the "scene" with the rebellious children of the sixties. It was the fashion not to have close family ties and solid marriages.

But before the family show broke up, we did have a chance to go on the road again, doing personal appearances throughout the United States — yes, in a Greyhound bus, doing one-nighters. And as we toured the country, we relived the band days of the forties and pointed out the old dance spots to our kids. A lot of the ballrooms are gone. The Frog Hop in St. Joseph, Missouri burned down. The Rainbow Rendezvous in Salt Lake City has given way to a high rise. The Paladium Ballroom in Hollywood still stands, but doesn't hold dances very often; it caters mostly to conventions. A lot of the ballrooms have been turned into roller rinks while some have just decayed with old age.

Our kids would say, "Mom, tell us about it. Tell us about the 'olden days.' "

And we would tell them how it was, touring with the big bands in those fabulous swinging years of the forties.

"This is where we played in Hershey, Pennsylvania, and rode that old roller coaster after the dance was over. And this is where the Valley Dale Ballroom was in Columbus, Ohio. Kay Starr was the girl singer with the Joe Venuti Band that played there just before we did."

We played there Christmas week, and I gave Alvino an electric train on Christmas Eve. When we invited the band up for eggnog, Alvino sulked because all the boys in the band kept playing with his train, and he didn't get a chance to touch it until they went home. It was a wonderful Christmas Eve in spite of our being on the road. All the band and the sisters were packed into one hotel room with a fragrant Christmas tree sitting on the dresser. We had to make the eggnog in the bathroom. Big snowflakes falling added to the Christmas spirit which we felt intensely even though all of us were far from home.

But now big bands are coming back. They really are. They are not just a memory. We have been hearing the rumor for so long, but now it is actually happening.

The older generation has started a rebellion, a quiet rebellion against the loud, violent rock sound. They recall those great old tunes of the thirties and the forties and have started requesting, even demanding them. The "oldies but goodies" are coming back on the radio. In every city in the United States, the old tunes are being played and we are hearing the big, beautiful sounds of the big bands.

As we go on tour doing our big band concerts every night, we look out over the audience and see a sea of white hair and glasses. One writer has called them the "cardiac sock hop set, the senior citizen swing set." Whatever you want to call them, they still have the enthusiasm of the kids of the forties, and it's a joy to perform for them.

We see a lot of changes on the road. After all, it has been forty years or more. Instead of staying in the heart of the city, we stay in motels in the suburbs. Instead of wandering around the city exploring and looking for exotic restaurants, we are now prisoners of Burger King and McDonalds. I see the young boys in our band dining on nothing but junk food, and I feel sorry for them. Will they ever be gourmets and enjoy the art of eating fine cuisine? I think not.

Of course, a lot of the big band leaders are gone, some retired or went into other businesses like Artie Shaw and Charlie Barnet. Others, like Tommy and Jimmie Dorsey and Glen Miller are gone. But a lot of them are still around. Les Brown, who had Bob Hope to support him in the lean band days, Woody Herman, and Bob Crosby, are as busy as they were in the forties.

Alvino is very active, doing one-nighters and personal appearances and concerts with his big band. All these band leaders are dusting off their old charts and are swinging like they did in the forties. They have discovered that not only old folks love them, but the young are beginning to discover and admire them as well. The college kids are again going wild over bands like Woody Herman, and Buddy Rich. Of course, the King of Swing, Benny Goodman, has never really left the scene. He is constantly in demand, appearing in concert with various symphonies and also with his sextette. And then there are the two all-time favorite bands, probably the greatest of them all according to many musicians — the bands of Duke Ellington and Count Basie. Duke died in 1974 but his son has carried on for him in leading the band.

And so the bands play on and gather momentum. Mozart wrote dance music and so did Strauss. Big band music is a part of history and a part of the American culture.

Artie Shaw who lectures on big band music and jazz said:

> "One of the few things I seem to get uptight about is the resentment of black musicians saying that white people took over their jazz. The angry militants say it was their music. And it was. But it would have remained 'Jelly Roll Morton' if whites hadn't gotten into it. Whites brought discipline to black music. There is plenty of reason for blacks to be angry, but you can't take hatred into music."

I think Shaw is right. There was no hatred or hidden messages in the music of our day. It was just the heartbeat of our glorious, romantic youth!

Our generation is tired of the beat of the drums and electronic sounds. We are tired of violence and harshness. We long for the sweetness and romance of the old movies, the old musicals of Broadway, and the wonderful old tunes we used to sing. We object to this wild, violent world we are living in, and we look back for romance, stability, and sweetness. I guess a lot of us are just sentimental slobs.

It's funny that out of those terrible war years of the forties, those hard, pitiful years of the Depression, those years that were so tough for most of us, we could glean such memories of music to enjoy now.

I guess the pain has been deadened and now all that is remembered is the sweetness. We were kids; we were young. We loved and laughed and lost and went on living again.

The Hotel Astor has been demolished and the Biltmore is getting a face lift to house the Bank of America. But they can't take away our music. May the bands play on!

After Lionel Hampton "wowed" them at a Reagan party, the President said:

"There are many ways people make contributions to their country . . . what you've done is make this country a happier place."

We're glad we grew up in the era of the big bands and that we, too, were able to make this country a happier place.

The 20s

Beginnings

Luise at seven years of age posing as a ballerina after starting ballet lessons at Christensen School of Dancing, forerunner of Ballet West

Daddy, Maxine, Mama, Baby Alyce, Karleton and Luise
just before moving to Ephraim

The Driggs family in Ephriam, Utah 1922
Alyce, Luise, Maxine & Karleton
Baby Yvonne and Baby Donna in front

The Driggs family of Entertainers
Our first performance without Mama and the two babies.
Santaquin, Utah 1922

Driggs family of Entertainers at the height of our concert tours
Back row: Luise,Mama, Daddy, Karleton, Maxine, Alyce
Front row: Yvonne, Billy, Donna
Glendale, California 1928

The Heidt Years

Moonlit Terrace
The Biltmore
NEW YORK

Cream Orienta
Stuffed Crab,
Half Cold Lo
Fresh Salmo
Crabmeat S
Fresh Shri
Lobster S
Terrine d 90
Boned C 1 35
Chicken ...ette 1 35

Paté de Foie-Gras 2 00
Assorted Cold Meats 1 25
Cold Meats with Chicken 1 50
Chicken Salad (White) 1 60
Chicken Salad (Dark) 90
Smoked Ox-tongue 90
Sugar Cured Ham 90
Virginia Ham 1 25
Westphalian Ham 1 25

SALADS

Romaine or Lettuce 50
Combination 50
Holland House 55
Biltmore 60
Hollywood 60
Tomato 50
Bird's Nest 50
Vegetable 60
De Luxe 60
Fruit 65
Alligator Pear 75

DINNER

...LAM JUICE COCKTAIL 45 SHRIMP COCKTAIL 75 TOMATO JUICE COCKTAIL 35
...tle Neck Clams 50 Cherrystone Clams 55 Cocktail Sauce 10
...ster Cocktail 1 25 Seafood Cocktail 1 10 Crab Meat Cocktail 85

...APEFRUIT SUPREME 70 OLIVES 35 RIPE 40 STUFFED 45 CELERY 35 STUFFED 45
...rted Hors d'Oeuvres 1 00 *(If Taken as an Only Course 1 50)* Scallions 25
...l Imported Beluga Caviar (P. P.) 2 25 Canapé 2 00 Radishes 25
...halian Ham 1 25 Smoked Salmon 70 Salami 55 Canapé of Anchovies 65
...r Pear Cocktail Biltmore 60 Fruit Cup Trianon 60 Antipasto Biltmore 65
Strawberry Cup with Kirsch 75

...INDIENNE 45 CONSOMME FLORIDA GAUFRETTES 45
...0 St. Germain 40 Petite Marmite Parisienne 60 Gumbo Creole 55
... or Gumbo Jelly 40 Beef or Chicken Consommé 35

...T OF SOLE, BONNE FEMME 1 15 BROILED SWORDFISH, FIGARO 1 00
KINGFISH SAUTE, ALLIANCE (10 M.) 1 15
CASSOLETTE OF LOBSTER, RICE MIRAMAR (10 M.) 1 60
SOFT SHELL CRABS 1 25 ENGLISH SOLE 1 25 P. P. FROG'S LEGS 1 50

ENTREES *(Ready)*
BRAISED OX-TONGUE, SPINACH, CROQUETTE POTATOES 1 40
BROILED BABY CHICKEN, BACON, O'BRIEN AU GRATIN 1 50
SCALLOPED SWEETBREAD UNDER BELL, BILTMORE 1 25
BEEF FILET MIGNON, BOUQUETIERE 1 80
COLD BONED CAPON, TOMATO VIRGINIA 1 40
SUPREME OF DUCKLING, SINGAPORE (15 M.) 1 75

ROASTS *(Ready)*
Prime Ribs of Beef 1 30 Hot House Baby Lamb 1 35
Half Roast Stuffed Spring Chicken 1 30

ROASTS *(To Order)*
BILTMORE BABY BROILER 1 50 *Guinea Chicken 4 00 JUMBO SQUAB 1 60
*Fresh Killed Broiler 2 25 Half 1 35 *Long Island Duckling 3 50 Half 2 00
Sirloin Steak (1) 2 15 Sirloin Steak (for 2) 4 00 Minute Steak 1 90 Filet Mignon 2 25

VEGETABLES
NEW CORN ON COB 45
NEW ASPARAGUS 1 00 NEW SWEET PEAS 55 LIMA BEANS 65 STRING BEANS 55
Artichoke 70 Broccoli 75 Cauliflower 55 Stuffed Green Pepper or Tomato 45
Fresh Mushrooms 80 Small Onions in Cream 50
Spinach 50 with Cream 55 Carrots Vichy 45 Celery au Jus 45
Beets in Butter 35 Squash 50 Oyster Bay Asparagus 80 Fried Egg Plant 40

POTATOES
MASHED 30 HASHED BROWNED 30 BOILED 25
AU GRATIN 30 SAUTE 30 BAKED IDAHO 35
Ideal 50 Anna 50 Soufflé 45 Lorette 45 Sweet Louisiana 45 Fried 30

DESSERTS
COLD DIPLOMAT PUDDING 40 MIXED FRUIT IN JELLY 40
STRAWBERRY SLICE 35
Stewed Fresh Strawberries 60 French Pastry 25 Frozen Puff Butterscotch Sauce 45
Green Apple Pie 35 Custard Pie 35
Cream Caramel 35 Port Wine Jelly with Fruit 45 Stewed Fresh Fruits 55
Terrace Layer Cake 30 Petit Fours 35 Crepes Suzette 1 00

ICE CREAM
CUP CARUSO 60 PROFITEROLE HELEN 50 RASPBERRIES PARISIENNE 60
Roly Foly 50 Tortoni 50 Nesselrode Pudding 55 Spumoni 45
Biscuit Glacé Terrace 45 Tutti Frutti 45 Floating Heart Creole 55
Burnt Almond, Pistache, Coffee, Chocolate, Vanilla, Strawberry 50
Water Ice—Raspberry, Lemon, Orange 40

CHEESE
ROQUEFORT 55 Imported Camembert 45 Swiss Cheese 45 BEL PAESE 45
Petit Gruyere 45 Port-du-Salut 45 Stilton 65 Gorgonzola 50
Cream Cheese 40 with Bar-le-Duc 55 Cottage Cheese with Cream 40

FRUIT
Huckleberries, Strawberries, Raspberries, Blackberries 55 with Cream 60
Cantaloupe 55 Watermelon 55
California Cherries 55 Apple 25 Pear 25 Grapes 55

Biltmore Coffee and Cream 35 Iced Coffee 40 Iced Tea 40
Demi-tasse 20 Tea 25 Acidophilus Milk 25 40

Bread and Butter 25 June 12, 1937

Star (*) Indicates Portion for Two

Cover Charge of $2.00 P. P. after 10 P. M.

Alvino Rey as he appeared when Luise first met him
San Francisco,Ca. 1933

The King Sisters and Horace Heidt, Chicago Theatre 1935
Donna, Yvonne, Luise, Alyce and Horace

Horace Heidt with the Alemite Brigadeers, the King Sisters and Alvino Rey
Yvonne, Donna, Luise, Alyce, Alvino, Horace, Lysbeth Hughes
Drake Hotel in Chicago 1935

Maid of honor
and bride

Alyce and Luise
May 21, 1937

Bride with her bridesmaids
Donna, Yvonne, Luise, Alyce May 21, 1937

Alvino and Luise in New York City 1937
Happy in their wedded life

King Sisters watch as Luise says goodbye to Alvino as sisters leave to do the Old Gold show with Artie Shaw in the summer of 1939

Five Mormon girls in Los Angeles in 1939
Donna, Laraine Day, Luise, Yvonne and Alyce discuss show business

SILVER FOREST

DINER MODERNE

Served from 6 p.m. to 9:30 p.m.

$2.50 per person

Choice

Fruit Supreme Grenadine — Stuffed Deviled Egg Russe
Chilled Pineapple or Tomato Juice
Cold Jellied Consomme — Fresh Crabmeat Cocktail
Consomme, Printaniere — Cream of Artichoke

Mixed Olives — Celery Hearts
Melba Toast — Saltine Crackers

Choice

Poached Chinook Salmon Court Bouillon Hollandaise Sauce
Brisket of Corned Beef with Cabbage or Leaf Spinach
Veal Steak Saute with Mushrooms and Tomato
Braised Boneless Leg of Lamb Vegetables Gravy
Cold Virginia Ham and Sliced Chicken, Spiced Pears

Our Chef Recommends
Mignon of Beef Tenderloin Saute Nemrod 3.00
Unjointed Butter Fried Chicken Maryland 2.75

New Spinach Souffle — Potatoes Fondantes
Steamed Zucchini Cream Sauce — Candied Sweet Potatoes

Hearts of Lettuce — Fedora Salad

Cheese and Crackers — Individual Apple Pie
Homemade Cake — Stewed Peaches
Banana Bavarian Cream
Choice of Ice Cream or Sherbet — Strawberry Sundae

Coffee Tea Milk

a Dessert worthy of your consideration
Drake Frozen Pudding Rum Sauce 35 cents

TODAY'S MENU

APPETIZERS
Cotuit Cocktail 55 — Blue Point Cocktail 50
Fruit Supreme Grenadine 75 — Stuffed Deviled Egg Russe 75
Fresh Crabmeat Cocktail 80 — Tomato or Pineapple Juice 30

SOUPS (Cup 35 Tureen 50)
Jellied Consomme, — Consomme, Printaniere
Chicken Okra Creole — Cream of Artichoke
Onion Soup au Gratin (15 minutes) 60 — Green Turtle Olorosso Cup 65

FISH
Fried Oysters Cape Cod Style 75 — Grilled Baby Lobster Drawn Butter 2.00
Cold Boiled Baby Lobster, Mayonnaise Half 1.00, Whole 1.75
Poached Salmon Court Bouillon Hollandaise Sauce 90
Baked Red Snapper Louisiannа 90

ENTREES
Unjointed Butter Fried Chicken Maryland 1.50
Breast of Guinea Hen under Bell Eugenie 1.50
Mignon of Beef Tenderloin Saute Nemrod 2.50
Veal Steak Saute with Mushrooms and Tomato, New Peas 1.50
Brisket of Corned Beef with Cabbage or New Spinach, Boiled Potato 1.25

OUR CHEF RECOMMENDS
Mignon of Beef Tenderloin Saute Nemrod: Saute in Butter Garnished with Chicken Dumpling, Sherry Wine and Fresh Mushroom Sauce 2.50

ROASTS
Roast Ribs of Prime Beef 1.25 extra cut 1.95
Roast Young Turkey with Dressing Cranberry Sauce 1.25

FRESH VEGETABLES
New Corn on Cob 40 — Corn Saute 50 — Plain New Spinach 40
New Green Peas 50 — Brussels Sprouts 50 — New String Beans 50

POTATOES
au Gratin Potatoes 40 — French Fried Potatoes 35
Candied Sweet Potatoes 40 — Baked Potato 40 — Potato Lyonnaise 40

SALADS
Hearts of Lettuce 40 — Lettuce and Tomato 50

TODAY'S SPECIAL: Fedora Salad: in Lettuce Basket, Slices of Apple and Oranges Covered with Mayonnaise, Decorated with Red Beets and Green Peppers 65

DESSERTS
Stewed Peaches 35 — Banana Bavarian Cream 25 — Strawberry Sundae 40
Sherbet 30 Ice Cream 35 — Homemade Cake 20 — Individual Apple Pie 25
Cantaloupe 30 Mode 50 — Persian Melon 40 — Assorted French Pastry 25
Honey Dew 40 — Fresh Strawberries or Raspberries 40 with Cream 50

CHEESE
Imported Roquefort 40 Camembert 35 Liederkranz 35 Philadelphia Cream .35

BEVERAGES
Demi Tasse 20 Milk 20 Coffee with Cream, Pot for One 25 Percolator 45
Cocoa or Chocolate Whipped Cream for One 35 — Fresh Buttermilk 20
Half and Half: per glass .35 — Orange Pekoe, Russian Caravan or Darjeeling 25

For Other Dishes Consult a la Carte Menu — Monday, September 28th

The 40s

Those Swinging Years

The King Sisters and the Alvino Rey Band at the Rustic Cabin in 1941

Band: Back row: Buddy Cole, piano, Sandy Bloch, bass, Icky Morgan, guitar, Bunny Shawker, drums, 2nd row: Danny Vanelli, trumpet, Frankie Strasseck, trumpet, Paul Fredricks, trumpet 3rd row: Wally Barron, trombone, Jerry Rosa, trombone Front row Bill Shine, sax, Jerry Sanfino, sax, Skeets Herfurt, sax, Kermit Levinsky, sax.

Alyce, Luise, Donna, Yvonne, June Havoc, Alvino at RKO
in 1941 movie, "Sing Your Worries Away"

King Sisters Luise, Donna, Alyce, Yvonne pose with Dean Jagger for 1941 picture

Buddy Ebsen and Yvonne try their hand at jitterbugging at RKO
in 1941 movie, "Sing Your Worries Away"

King Sisters Alyce, Luise, Donna and Yvonne at RKO
in Hollywood 1941

Alvino Rey in the summer of 1942 New York City

Luise King in the summer of 1942 New York City

A TRADE SERVICE FEATURE OF Billboard

The Billboard

WEEK ENDING FEBRUARY 20, 1942

MUSIC POPULARITY CHART

NATIONAL AND REGIONAL BEST SELLING RETAIL RECORDS

NATIONAL

POSITION Last Wk.	This Wk.	
5	1.	MOONLIGHT COCKTAIL —GLENN MILLER Bluebird 11401
1	2.	A STRING OF PEARLS —GLENN MILLER Bluebird 11382
[illegible]	3.	DEEP IN THE HEART OF TEXAS —ALVINO REY Bluebird 11391
2	4.	I SAID NO —ALVINO REY Bluebird 11391
3	5.	BLUES IN THE NIGHT —WOODY HERMAN Decca 4030
6	6.	REMEMBER PEARL HARBOR —SAMMY KAYE Victor 27738
4	7.	BLUES IN THE NGHT —JIMMIE LUNCEFORD Decca 4125
—	8.	ROSE O'DAY —KATE SMITH Columbia 36448
10	9.	WHITE CLIFFS OF DOVER —GLENN MILLER Bluebird 11397
—	10.	I DON'T WANT TO WALK WITHOUT YOU —HARRY JAMES Columbia 36478

EAST

POSITION Last Wk.	This Wk.	
3	1.	Moonlight Cocktail —Glenn Miller
5	2.	Remember Pearl Harbor —[illegible] Kaye
2	3.	I Said No —Alvino Rey
[illegible]	4.	[illegible] —Jimmie Lunceford
10	5.	Rose O'Day —Kate Smith
6	6.	A String of Pearls —Glenn Miller
1	7.	Blues in the Night —Woody Herman
—	8.	Blues in the Night —Cab Calloway
—	9.	Deep in the Heart of Texas—Alvino Rey
—	10.	I Don't Want To Walk Without You —Harry James

MIDWEST

POSITION Last Wk.	This Wk.	
7	1.	Deep in the Heart of Texas—Alvino Rey
3	2.	[illegible] —Glenn Miller
—	3.	Moonlight Cocktail —Glenn Miller
10	4.	Blues in the Night —Woody Herman
2	5.	Rose O'Day —[illegible]
[illegible]	6.	I Said No—Alvino Rey
[illegible]	7.	White Cliffs of D[illegible] —Kate Smith

SOUTH

POSITION Last Wk.	This Wk.	
1	1.	A String of Pearls —Glenn Miller
6	2.	Moonlight Cocktail —Glenn Miller
2	3.	Blues in the Night —Woody Herman
7	4.	Deep in the Heart of Texas—Alvino Rey
3	5.	Remember Pearl Harbor —Sammy Kaye
8	6.	Blues in the Night —Dinah Shore
5	7.	White Cliffs of Dover —Glenn Miller
—	8.	Blues in the Night —Cab Calloway
—	9.	Deep in the Heart of Texas—Bing Crosby
—	10.	I Don't Want To Walk Without You—H. James

WEST COAST

POSITION Last Wk.	This Wk.	
10	1.	Moonlight Cocktail —Glenn Miller
[illegible]	2.	I Said No—Alvino Rey
2	3.	Blues in the Night —Jimmie Lunceford
—	4.	White Cliffs of Dover —Glenn Miller
6	5.	Deep in the Heart of Texas—Alvino Rey
—	6.	How About You? —Tommy Dorsey
5	7.	A String of Pearls —Glenn Miller
—	8.	I Don't Want To Walk

The Nelson-Hilliard domestic tangles, CBS are musically backed by the King Sisters

Rey Band Dashes to Coast and Lolls for Week As Movie Becomes Big Hit Before It's Made

Making Of "Sing Your Worries Away" Is Perfect Example of Hollywood Process

CEDAR GROVE, N. J.—Now appearing at the Meadowbrook, Alvino Rey and his cohorts have an inside story about how fast Hollywood really works.

Their new picture hits the screen in February. When they arrived in L. A. to make it a few months ago, after a non-stop trip out from Philadelphia, they were told to wait a week—RKO hadn't made any definite decision on the story yet.

During that week the story was set and the director (Eddie Sutherland) was chosen (on the last day). The picture itself was taken out of the "B" class (second half of a double feature) and made an "A" picture (so "Sing Your Worries Away" will appear in all the top run houses) before a single camera rolled.

At Least They Exercised

The Four King Sisters spent two days rehearsing a strenuous dance routine with four partners. Even though Alyce and Louise were professional dancers a few years ago, it was tough going. Just as they got it down pat the number was tossed out of the picture.

The Rey band was held over an additional week beyond their contract when, at the last minute, a special production number featuring Eddie Julian on the drums was decided upon.

Alvino Rey surrounded by the lovely King Sisters in a scene from RKO's "Sing Your Worries Away", their forthcoming movie musical.

Coincidence met Alvino on the RKO lot. He's a radio fan, and for the past few years has been in radio communications with a fellow on the coast. Neither knew the other's name, just his short wave identification number.

Fancy Meeting You

While Al was working on "Sing Your Worries Away" he got into some radio "shop talk" with the sound technician. They discussed short wave mention numbers, and found (at that late date) that they were the two who had been carrying on a transcontinental short wave conversation.

Jack Egan, the band's manager, press agent, stage production specialist, and writer for the opera that he acts the part of commentator in (on the stage) also met a friend, Cliff Reid, who

King Sisters, Romance, And Stars Meet In L. A.

CEDAR GROVE, N. J.—The King Sisters' recollections of their

Kirby
Krupa
Alvino Rey
Carter
Basie
Goodman
Higgenbotham
Williams
Barnet

King Sisters Donna, Luise, Alyce, Yvonne
pose with Les Brown at the Paladium
in November of 1943

Alvino Rey with the Alvino Rey Band and the King Sisters
pack them in at the Meadowbrook in 1942

Alvino Rey in tails
tailored by Jonah
Luise King in gown
designed by Universal's
Vera Maxwell
Paladium Ballroom
1942

King Sisters Yvonne, Donna, Alyce, Luise
dig Tommy Dorsey at the Paladium 1945

King Sisters with their babies but Luise still without
Yvonne and Tina Cole, Donna and Candy Conkling, Luise,
Alyce and Lex de Azevedo

King sisters with babies--now Luise has children of her own
Candy, Donna, Jamie, Rick, Alyce, Lex, Rob, Liza, Luise
and Cathy, Yvonne and Tina

Left to right: Mr. & Mrs. Buddy Cole, Mr. & Mrs. Alvino Rey, Mr. and Mrs. Syd de Azevedo Mr. and Mrs. Jim Conkling. Picture taken at the Paladium in October 1945 when Alvino and Syd were on leave

Los Angeles Times

RECORDS

THE EXPERTS PICK The All-Time Greats!

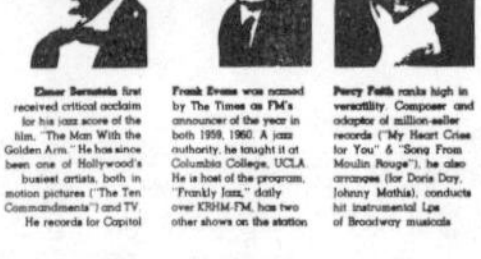

by WALLY GUENTHER

Elmer Bernstein first received critical acclaim for his jazz score of the film, "The Man With the Golden Arm." He has since been one of Hollywood's busiest artists, both in motion pictures ("The Ten Commandments") and TV. He records for Capitol

Frank Evans was named by The Times as FM's announcer of the year in both 1959, 1960. A jazz authority, he taught it at Columbia College, UCLA. He is host of the program, "Frankly Jazz," daily over KRHM-FM, has two other shows on the station

Percy Faith ranks high in versatility. Composer and adaptor of million-seller records ("My Heart Cries for You" & "Song From Moulin Rouge"), he also arranges (for Doris Day, Johnny Mathis), conducts hit instrumental Lps of Broadway musicals

● What would be your answer if asked to name the all-time great recording personalities?

That's the question we posed to Home magazine's six-man panel. Their answers indicate one of two things: either the experts have relatively short memories, or records have never been better.

For all nine winners named best in their field are active today. Most are at the peak of their careers. Not one legendary name from the past managed to garner enough votes to lead in any of the categories.

● The winners:

Ella Fitzgerald, popular and jazz vocalist (female); Frank Sinatra, popular vocalist (male); Joe Williams, jazz singer (male); Count Basie, big band; George Shearing, small instrumental group; Hi-Los, vocal group (male); King Sisters, vocal group (female); Andre Kostelanetz, mood music.

They were selected by a consensus vote of panel members Elmer Bernstein, Frank Evans, Percy Faith, Henry Mancini, Nelson Riddle and Dick Whittinghill, all of whom are actively involved in the music and recording industries.

Balloting was limited to nine categories in covering an admittedly wide area. Therefore, the selections did not come easy. For the panel members—like everyone else—possess strong, individual and ... preferences.

... gerald, was also the ... on all six ballots as ... utpointed her rivals ... ressive. ... rnstein) ... "Ella ... he's No. 1 in both ... ank Sinatra, who ... male pops singer. ... h) ... "The great- ... d the greatest in- ... and knows how to ... utstanding ..." ... d category. Here ... on, Benny Good- ... Basie edging past ... final choice im- ... ined such a high ... thankful ..." ... were named on ... up (listed alphabetically) were:

Popular vocalist (female): Rosemary Clooney, Doris Day, Peggy Lee, Carmen McRae, Patti Page, Kate Smith, Jo Stafford, Kay Starr.

Jazz vocalist (female): Pearl Bailey, June Christy, Rosemary Clooney, Billie Holiday, Peggy Lee, Anita O'Day, Bessie Smith, Lee Wiley.

Popular singer (male): David Allen, Harry Belafonte, Nat Cole, Perry Como, Bing Crosby, Vic Damone, Dick Haymes, Johnny Mathis.

Vocal group (female): Andrews Sisters, Clark Sisters, DeCastro Sisters, McGuire Sisters.

HOME MAGAZINE'S ALL-TIME RECORD GREATS

Popular vocalist (female)	Ella Fitzgerald
Jazz vocalist (female)	Ella Fitzgerald
Popular vocalist (male)	Frank Sinatra
Jazz vocalist (male)	Joe Williams
Big band	Count Basie
Small group	George Shearing
Vocal group (male)	Hi-Los
✓ Vocal group (female)	King Sisters
Mood music	Andre Kostelanetz

Henry Mancini can thank TV for his top successes. Veteran film composer, he shot to prominence with the striking theme music for Peter Gunn, repeated success with score for Mr. Lucky. His Gunn album is nearing 1 million sales, a rarity for instrumentals

Nelson Riddle discarded a trombone for arranging in the late 40s, and has since risen steadily to the top of his field. His work has sparked success of many hits, including those by Nat (King) Cole and Frank Sinatra. Riddle is also active in films, TV music

Dick Whittinghill is one of the Southland's most popular radio figures. His morning KMPC show is a slick mixture of music, mirth anchored by a solid knowledge of music dating to stints with the Four Esquires, Pied Pipers vocal groups

32

BRENT WILSON / personal management

5216 fulton avenue • sherman oaks • california

APRIL 6, 1959 THE BILLBOARD MUSIC 11

The King Sisters

BEST PERFORMANCE BY A VOCAL GROUP or CHORUS

"Imagination"—Album

Capitol

NOMINATED by the awards committee of the National Academy of Recording Arts and Sciences

'58 NARAS AWARDS '58

Our Most Humble Thanks to the NARAS for this Greatest of Honors!

Current Single
"KEEP SMILING"
b/w "MAIDS OF CADIZ"

Current L.P.'s
"IMAGINATION"
"ALOHA"

Soon to be released
"WARM AND WONDERFUL"

Capitol

... also thanks to those without whose help this could not have happened—

Alvino Rey · Warren Barker · Roy Chamberlain

... and for the fabulous T.V. presentation Steve Allen gave us on the title tune ... (and you too—L. G.)

Personal Management
Brent Wilson
5216 Fulton Ave., Sherman Oaks, Calif.

The Mormon Sisters Swing It

But 4 King Girls Have No Other Vices

By EARL WILSON

NO COFFEE, TEA, CIGGIES NOR ALKY

Post Photos

DONNA, LOUISE, ALYCE AND YVONNE KING, Mormons from Salt Lake City, who are trying to capture Broadway although living up to Joseph Smith's Word of Wisdom, too.

As soon as the reporter sagged down at the table to lunch with the four Mormon sisters who are here to sing and swing their way to fame, he smiled winningly and said: "Cocktails?"

"Oh," came a nervous but very firm reply from Alyce, the 24-year-old one, "we don't drink. We have drunk tea a couple of times, but only for medicinal purposes. Like when I had a larnyx condition, I had a couple of cups, with lemon. That wasn't sinning."

"Uhh-h-h," said the reporter, "cigarette?"

"Asthma cigarettes," quickly put in Donna, the 21-year-old one, "are the only kind we approve, and none of us has asthma. Our grandmother, who went across the plains in a covered wagon, blew smoke in my ear once for an earache, but that's as near as I ever got to smoking. We feel it is no more difficult for us not to smoke than it is for you to smoke."

For Amusement

"I see," said the interxiewer. "What do you girls do to amuse yourselves?"

"Our dad," replied Yvonne, the 19-year-old, very blonde one, "is quite a philospher and a wonderful writer. He sends us sermons and we read them to members of the Alvino Rey dance band, in which we are partners."

"Yes," spoke up Laure, the 25-year-old one, proudly, "Alvino Rey is my husband. He"—she smiled happily"is a Christian Scientist."

Clearly, the King Sisters from Salt Lake City, newest rivals of the Boswell Sisters and the Andrews Sisters, are modern miracles. They're nieces of Sen. William H. King, and granddaughters of Perley P. Pratt, one of the early Mormons who was murdered for his faith. They're currently trying to conquer Broadway by singing jive while never departing from the word of Wisdom which Joseph Smith said he saw in a vision in 1853. The Word of Wisdom bans tobacco, alcohol and hot liquids.

"We are going into the Paramount May 7," said Yvonne, who handles the publicity for the team, "so you see we haven't hurt ourselves any by stressing any by stressing the Word of Wisdom in our personal lives.

Only Four Grandparents

"We are real Mormons," she continued. "Both our grandfathers had two wives at the same time. We know for a fact that it was all carried out in decent fashion and that it was only because they thought it was a law straight from God that they did it. Our parents think that all four of our grandparents——"

"You mean all six of your grandparents."

"All four! We don't count those extra wives. Anyway, our parents think all four of our grandparents did perfectly right at the time."

As most everybody knows, polygamy hasn't been a part of Mormonism since last century, so the King Sisters said they thought it should be made clear that there is no polygamy afoot in the 21-room house which they share with members of the Alvino Rey band at Englewood Cliffs, N. J., on Palisades Av. The band and its sister team of vocalists appear regularly at the Rustic Cabin, on Route 9W, near Englewood, and so the whole company of about 15 pours into the big house every 3 a. m.

Laura Is a Chaperon

"Another wife and I are the chaperons," said Laura, the married one. "There has been no romance except between Vonnie and Buddy Cole, the pianist."

"He was sort of her love out on the coast," put in Donna hastily.

"In a school held by our church," explained Vonnie, "we studied cooking, dancing, how to be charming, how to get your man, and we even discussed sex, all in a very wholesome, constructive way, but this is more a business partnership.

"When we get home, it's a free-for-all. Everybody cooks. The boys come in their tuxedos and stand in line at the stove with their little frying pans. Later they wash their little dishes and pans. We each have our own room. We have two short-wave sending sets, a Hammond organ, a reed organ, a movie machine and voice-recording machine, and two pianos. We girls tell each other off something awful. If one walks ahead, we'll say, 'Look at her, she walks like a cow.' It makes us all more careful."

"The Picknickiest Family"

"And," said Alyce, "we're the picknickiest family. For Christmas, I got a lunch basket, with dishes."

Recently the girls turned down a fat radio offer from a tobacco company because the contract would have required them to sign a testimonial saying they liked a certain brand, whereas they've never smoked.

When they were asked what company laid down such a requirement, Vonnie disclosed that her Mormonism has a rival, Winchellism. "Just say," said this grand-daughter of the Mormon martyrs, "that it was a ciggie commercial."

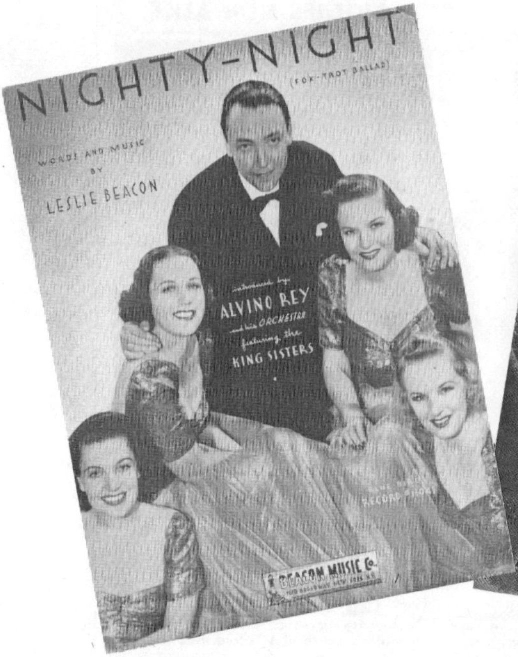

NIGHTY-NIGHT
(FOX-TROT BALLAD)
WORDS AND MUSIC
BY
LESLIE BEACON
introduced by
ALVINO REY
and his ORCHESTRA
featuring the
KING SISTERS
BEACON MUSIC Co.

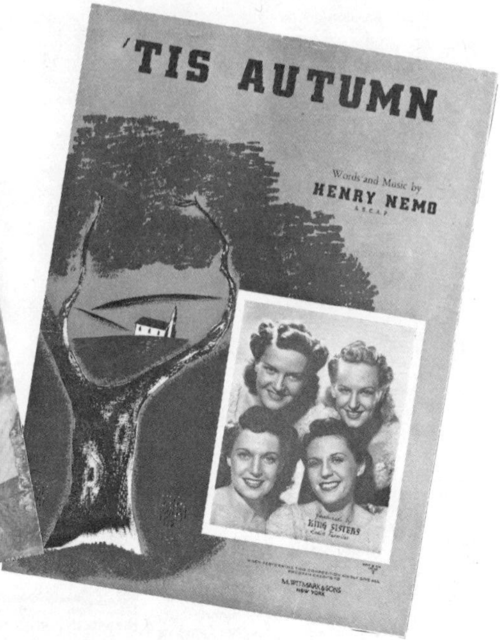

'TIS AUTUMN
Words and Music by
HENRY NEMO
A.S.C.A.P.
KING SISTERS
M. WITMARK & SONS
NEW YORK

The 50s

Rebuilding

King Sisters at Harrah's Club in Lake Tahoe 1957
Yvonne, Alyce, Luise, Marilyn

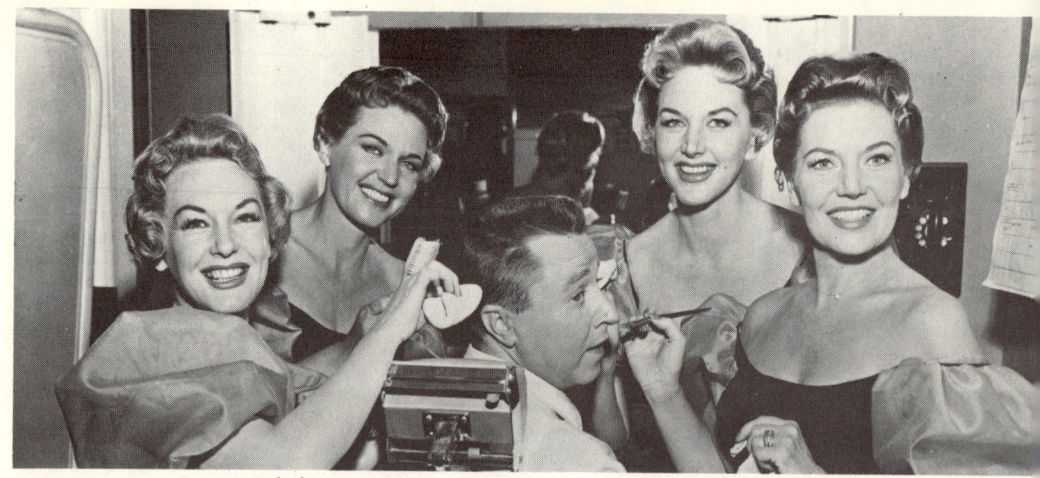
George Gobel poses with Yvonne, Luise, Marilyn and Alyce 1956 in Hollywood

King Sisters in Hollywood 1957 Yvonne, Alyce, Luise, Marilyn

King Sisters and Steve Allen
Hollywood 1958

King Sisters appear with Meredith Willson at Hollywood Bowl
The girls are wearing gowns designed by sister Maxine
Meredith Willson, Rene Willson, Marilyn, Luise, Alyce, Yvonne, Roy Chamberlain

Back row: Bill, LaVarn, Kent, Alvino, Bill, Bob, Jim, Karleton. Second row: Donna, Maxine, Yvonne, Luise, Marilyn, Alyce, Hazel, Phyllis . Third row: Carolyn, Jon, Rick, Lex, Bill,Don, Ray, Jamie, Liza. Front row: Xan, Candy, Adam, Volney, Laurette, Cam, Jennie, Susannah, Steve, Debbie, Tina, Jonathan

The 60s

The First Family of Television

The King family in the Old Dodge touring car done up Hollywood style at the beginning of the family television series in 1965

Mothers Day with the King Family TV special May 1968

1966 Christmas party at the home of Mr. & Mrs. Bill Harrah in Lake Tahoe when family played Harrah's Club. Back row: Tina, Cathy, Bob, Rob, Alvino, Kent, Don, Jim, Bill, Phyllis, Tommy, Jamie, Lex, Xandra, Chris, Candy. Front row: Luise, Alyce, Yvonne, Mr. & Mrs. Harrah, Del, Maxine, LaVarn, Donna. Seated on floor: Ray, Marilyn, Jon, Rick

King mothers and daughters on Christmas TV special 1967
Left to right: Yvonne, Burch, Tina Cole, Maxine Thomas, Candy Conkling, Alyce Clarke, Carolyn Thomas
Donna Conkling, Cathy Cole, Luise Rey, Jamie Conkling, Marilyn Larsen, Lize Rey

July 1975. The King Family Touring Group. Thunderbird Hotel in Las Vegas.
Rick, Tina, Rob, Yvonne, Bob, Alyce, Alvino, Luise, Kent, Laurette, Jon,
Carolyn, Volney, Marilyn, Cathy, Cam, Brian, Jenny, Jamie

The 70s and 80s

Still Going Strong

King Sisters as they appear today as mothers and grandmothers
Still going strong

Johnnie Smith (one of the Ink Spots), Luise, Connie Haines
On the road again with the Big Band Show 1981

California Utah Women

Women Proud of Their Heritage

Utah Chapter

April 23, 1983

Mrs. Luise King Rey
10275 South 2505 East
Sandy, Utah 84092

Dear Luise:

California Utah Women of Utah and the 500 guests who enjoyed the April 16th luncheon/fashion show at the Hotel Utah salute the King Sisters for such quality entertainment.

Members of the board have received compliments on your classic styling, the warm and ingenious way you have of making an audience feel close, and the refined manner in delivering a selection of songs that gave rise to nostalgic happy reminiscing done by the most pleasing voices in the business.

The sharing of your special talents, and the giving of your valuable time was a great contribution to the success of the afternoon. Thank you, too, for the lovely records you donated. We appreciate and love you.

Most cordially,

Marjorie Lee

Marjorie Lee,
Corresponding Secretary

Shown above: Yvonne, Alyce, Luise, Marilyn

Yvonne Burch: Yvonne is married to William Burch, recently released vice president of MCA. She is enjoying condominium living in Palm Springs. She has two daughters and four grandchildren

Alyce Clarke: A member of the original trio, Alyce is married to Robert Clarke, a film actor in Hollywood where she still lives. She has three sons and nine grandchildren

Luise Rey: One of the original King Sisters trio. Has been married to Alvino Rey for 45 years and they are far from being retired. They are, to quote Luise, "as busy as we want to be." Luise can be persuaded to sing an occasional solo with Alvino's band. They have three children and five grandchildren.

Marilyn Larsen: Prominent during the King Family Television Show, Marilyn's husband, Kent, sang and played jazz trombone with the Stan Kenton Band. Since his death Marilyn has lived in the San Fernando Valley and performs often. She has three children and her two daughters serve as her back up singers when they are in town.

Donna Conkling: Donna left show business in the 50s to raise her family now consisting of five children. She is married to Jim Conkling and lives in Agoura, California. They have fifteen grandchildren.

Maxine Thomas: The eldest and one of the three original singers. When she left to get married, Donna began her singing career. Maxine designed the King Sisters gowns for many years. She is married to LaVarn Thomas. They have two children and six grandchildren.

Aboard S.S. Independence on Hawaiian cruise, the Alvino Rey Band makes music and Luise spends her afternoon with Mr. and Mrs. Cary Grant. Summer 1983

Alvino today

Luise today